D0810358

LINGUISTICS AND
TEACHING
FOREIGN LANGUAGES

LINGUISTICS AND TEACHING FOREIGN LANGUAGES

Eric H. Kadler

Lycoming College

Van Nostrand Reinhold Company

New York   Cincinnati   Toronto   London   Melbourne

Van Nostrand Reinhold Company Regional Offices:
Cincinnati   New York   Chicago   Millbrae   Dallas

Van Nostrand Reinhold Company Foreign Offices:
London   Toronto   Melbourne

Published by Van Nostrand Reinhold Company
450 West 33rd Street, New York, N. Y. 10001

Published simultaneously in Canada by
D. Van Nostrand Company (Canada), Ltd.

10   9   8   7   6   5   4   3   2   1

To Karen and Marcia

PREFACE

This book is intended as a contribution to the professional preparation of foreign-language teachers. Toward this goal, the emphasis is not only on the mastery of the language alone but also on the proper understanding of linguistic principles. Those concerned with language-teaching methodology largely agree that there is ". . . a need either to include courses in linguistics on a college level for future language teachers, or else to require *all* teachers of languages to have at least one additional year of linguistic training before going into the profession."[1]

In writing this book I sought to provide language majors and language teachers with information that will go hand-in-hand with the rest of their training. The text is based on years of experimentation, and the material has proved challenging and valuable to students regardless of the specific languages they were preparing to teach.

A number of men and women who are now teaching French, German, Russian, or Spanish at all levels helped to shape the material in its present form. It is also my pleasure to acknowledge the assistance of many colleagues, notably S. R. Brost, Guy Mentha, and Leo Winston, whose experience and suggestions are reflected in different chapters of the book. My special thanks go to Francis L. Bayer for his constructive evaluation of the material on language analysis.

No one has ever written a text without a debt to his predecessors in the field. I expressly recognize Robert Lado and Robert L. Politzer, who were among my teachers at the University of Michigan.

Eric H. Kadler

[1] A. F. Gut, "A Survey of Methods and Materials in French Language Programs of American Colleges and Universities," *The Modern Language Journal*, LI no. 8 (Dec. 1967), 479.

CONTENTS

INTRODUCTION

Professional instruction in foreign languages has abandoned much of its former permissive amateurism and has now entered a phase of rigorous professionalism. Increasingly, American institutions of higher education are called upon to produce graduates who can effectively teach the foreign languages they have studied. Naive assumptions about foreign-language learning are challenged as never before, and the foreign-language teacher can now speak with professional authority in his own field and from a new position of influence. While there is much diversity of opinion regarding the training that will produce an excellent language teacher, there is general agreement that he should study some linguistics. A committee acting on behalf of the Modern Language Association of America describes one aspect of his qualifications as follows:

> The excellent foreign language teacher knows about the nature of language in general and he is able to use with some ease the major tools that have been developed for analyzing and describing language. In particular, he has had some training in applying these tools to the language he is teaching and he therefore has some understanding of its elements and structure — from the totality of an entire speech utterance down to its individual sounds. In his acquisition of this knowledge, he has given specific attention to contrastive linguistics, a closely related body of knowledge which analyzes the similarities and differences between the design of the foreign language and the design of English, the mother tongue of the vast majority of his students. This aspect of contrastive linguistics is, of course, important for American foreign language teachers whose mother tongue is not English; it is, however, equally important for language teachers who are native speakers of English.

Above all, the excellent foreign language teacher understands enough about linguistic science to know how it is related to his work and what the language teaching profession may learn from it. Linguistics is not to him — as it is to many uninformed language teachers — a vast unknown land peopled by creatures who speak gibberish to one another and who occasionally leave their esoteric labors to point an accusing finger at the language teaching profession. Hostility has given way to understanding and tolerance, as language teachers have learned more about the field of linguistics.

The language teacher who has had even minimal training in linguistics — if this training has been at all adequate — understands why it is that in a science so young, no unified theory has yet emerged that satisfies everyone. The Galileos have, however, already come and gone; and because great progress is currently being made, change in linguistic theory is uncomfortably rapid. This is of course confusing to the practitioner. But the informed teacher understands why this apparent confusion is normal in this period of the development of a science.

... The informed language teacher knows that this is the price of progress in any science and he does not allow this natural state of affairs to disturb him. He knows that the theories formulated today are not the final ones; they will give way to better ones tomorrow and he will have to learn those too. But above all, his work in linguistics has helped him brush away the centuries of accumulated myth that our culture has inherited about the nature of language, about particular languages and dialects, and about the sounds, words, and structures of the foreign language he is teaching.[1]

A person who speaks and perhaps even teaches several languages is not necessarily a linguist. Such a person is polylingual and may be called a polyglot. Nor does being a speaker of several languages make one an expert teacher of those languages any more than it makes him a linguist.

A person who studies ancient texts and their language or who is concerned with the development of ancient languages, such as Sanscrit,

---

[1] Reprinted by permission of the Modern Language Association from Joseph Axelrod, *The Education of the Modern Foreign Language Teacher for American Schools* (MLA, 1966).

is today called a philologist, rather than a linguist. A linguist in the contemporary sense is a social scientist engaged in the task of analyzing and classifying the spoken language of a given social or ethnic group. If he concerns himself with the description of the structure of one language alone, he is a descriptive or structural linguist. In most cases, however, he may also be referred to as a comparative linguist, because his work will necessarily involve the comparison of relationships or contrasts between the structures of at least two languages. This, of course, is only a very simplified clarification of the concepts involved.

There is no denying that the uncovering of basic linguistic units through the application of rigorous linguistic methods has given us greater insight into the systematic structure of language. Terms such as *phoneme, allophone, morpheme, suprasegmental phoneme,* and others, have not been invented to confuse laymen but to facilitate communication among linguists and language teachers.

Linguistic analysis, furthermore, can reveal to the language teacher essential structural differences between the source language (the native tongue of the learner) and the target language being taught. The recognition of and familiarity with these differences is important for the language teacher, for it helps him highlight the major difficulties of teaching a given language. Only if he is aware of these differences or points of conflict, as they are called, can he stress the features of the target language that require extra learning effort.

This book is an attempt to give the foreign-language teacher a panoramic knowledge of linguistics as applied to teaching techniques. Along with Charles C. Fries, the author insists that one can achieve sufficient mastery of the techniques of linguistic analysis and be a good practitioner in analyzing and describing languages without becoming a specialist in linguistic science.

Chapters 1 to 4 offer the basics of general linguistics. They represent a practical introduction to articulatory phonetics, the study of producing speech sounds; to phonemics, the study of distinctive sound features within a language; to morphemics, the study of units of meaning; and to a new analysis of syntax, the study of meaningful arrangements of such units. Each chapter includes a series of Review

Questions, which test the student's comprehension and retention of the salient points of each topic.

Chapters 5 and 6 give the teacher practical suggestions on how to recognize and deal with common language-learning problems in the area of pronunciation. The emphasis is on exercises with contrastive pairs. They are intended to help the student hear and produce the new sounds needed in our target languages: French, German, Russian, and Spanish — sounds that are problems because one gets along without them in English.

Description and practice of these sounds are combined. We feel that the usefulness of a good description is not denied by the truism that you cannot teach pronunciation by speaking about it. A student can be most easily taught the Spanish intervocalic **b**, for instance, by being told not to close his lips. Our aim has been to suggest the most practical devices that have been used successfully in the classroom.

Obviously, description of sounds and how they are produced cannot be a substitute for imitation of native or near-native speakers. Hence we included many examples of contrastive pairs which show how to focus the student's attention on specific sounds and how to overcome the interference of the native sound system.

Chapter 7 presents a brief discussion and a few basic samples of syntactic pattern drills. The theory of pattern drills has been explained in many publications and put into practice in the exercises of almost every recent textbook. Series of pattern drills of all shapes and sizes are now available in books such as Etmekjian's *Pattern Drills in Language Teaching* (see Bibliography).

The overall objective of our presentation is to encourage students to look into other sources of topical materials. The first five chapters include a list of suggested readings on identical or related topics in several books and professional journals.

The student who is getting ready to teach knows that learning a foreign language requires a lot of work. Effective teaching of languages is no less demanding. This book was written to make that demanding work more interesting, efficient, and professional.

LINGUISTICS AND
TEACHING
FOREIGN LANGUAGES

1

MODES OF COMMUNICATION

Broadly speaking, language is a complex system of communication, within which we can discern three modes or areas:

Speech
Writing
Paralanguage

Paralanguage   This mode of communication, almost international in its use, is restricted to relatively rare communication situations. Some of its common uses occur in regulating vehicular traffic (the international road-sign code), in the semaphore alphabet (the use of flags), in the sign language of the deaf and dumb, and in facial as well as acoustic but nonlingual expressions of joy, sadness, praise, or disapproval. A wink of the eye, tears, smiles, gesticulating, nodding as well as stamping feet, clapping hands, whistling, booing, and other nonspeech sounds are considered paralanguage. Some linguists claim that anything called paralanguage has to be audible, though not necessarily produced by vocal organs.[1] According to that theory, a message transmitted in the Morse code would be paralanguage only if the use of the code consisted of short and long sounds, not of dots and dashes. In practice, the audible and visual must occasionally combine to convey a message. For example, in a

---

[1] For a discussion of this theory see "Paralinguistics and Kinesics," by Alfred S. Hayes, in *Approaches to Semiotics* (The Hague: Mouton & Co., 1964), pp. 145–167.

large part of the Eastern Mediterranean there is a negative reply which consists of a click accompanied by a sharp lift of the head and eyebrows. The audible click is only a part of the paralinguistic "no."

It is not within the scope of this book to deal with the phenomena of paralanguage, but certain of its aspects should not be neglected by foreign-language teachers. The learning of meaningful facial expressions, gestures, and nonspeech sounds requires discrete imitation of life models. (Foreign films in our target languages are possible substitutes for life models.)

The science which deals with communicating by gestures and facial expressions is called *kinesics*. The word is derived from Greek *kinesi* — motion. The science of symbols and signs is called semeiology or *semiotics*. The word is derived from Greek *semeion* — sign.

Writing   This mode of communication represents a system of graphic symbols used by the literate members of a community to convey everyday messages (such as advertising) or to put down on paper ideas and words. This latter function of writing — so well exemplified by the work of Plato, who preserved in writing the words spoken by Socrates — has preserved for us the great thinking of the past. From the point of view of literature (*belles lettres*), writing as an art can exist without speech and occasionally it "influences the spoken language and induces changes in the overall structure of the system, some of which may be of major significance."[1]

Obviously, writing has a built-in permanence and need not rely on the support of kinesics and other paralinguistic phenomena. Many respected traditional grammar texts illustrate the proper use of spoken language by quotations from the writings of recognized authors.

The general study of writing systems is called graphetics, graphemics, or simply *graphics*. Some researchers prefer to use the term graphonomy, on the model of astronomy.

Depending on the type of graphic signs or symbols used in the sys-

---

[1] Albert Valdman, "On the Primacy of Writing in French: The Primacy of Speech," *The Modern Language Journal* L (Nov. 1966): 427.

tem, we distinguish two general groups of writing: (a) pictographic or ideographic, (b) syllabic and alphabetic.

Pictographic or ideographic writing depicts a whole concept by one particular symbol. The graphic symbols are not indicative of the sounds of the language and offer no clue to its pronunciation. On the other hand, their meanings are relatively easy to infer. The original writing of the Egyptians consisted of symbols called hieroglyphics (sacred carvings) and showed considerable realism:

The first hieroglyphic represents an eagle, the second a lioness, the third an owl, and the fourth a horned asp, an Egyptian venomous snake. (These pictographs are said to be the ancestors of our letters A, L, M, and U, respectively.)

In Chinese writing, "horse" is symbolized by a pictogram derived from what was originally a primitive picture of a horse. "East" is symbolized by a pictogram representing the sun, which is placed over the pictogram for a tree. The combination depicts an abstract concept (the East) and is preferably referred to as an ideogram.[1]

The realism of the original pictograms was gradually subdued in more complex ideograms, but the writing did not become simpler. An example is the Chinese pronoun *we*, which is written 𠮷 . It should be added, however, that modern China has started introducing a drastically simplified writing system.

Syllabic and alphabetic writings are characterized by graphic symbols (letters) for a single concept (word). The graphic symbols are relatively few but can be used in an infinite number of combinations. The symbols of a syllabic system of writing form its syllabary. The Japanese and the Ethiopians thus do not have an alphabet, but a

[1] I am indebted for this information to Mario Pei, *Invitation to Linguistics* (New York: Doubleday, 1965), p. 24.

syllabary. Their writing systems allow for the use of one written symbol as a syllable, which may consist of two or more sounds. This does not mean, however, that every symbol of a syllabary represents a syllable. Some of the symbols can mark a single vowel or a single consonant. The following are a few symbols of the Old Persian syllabary, which influenced other syllabic writings:

	ka		ga		ba		a
	ku		gu		mi		i

Our alphabet (the Latin alphabet) and other alphabets — such as the original German (Gothic) and the Cyrillic used in Russian and a few East European languages — are historically derived from the Greek alphabet, which is still used in modern Greek. The Greek alphabet, in its turn, developed from the symbols of the Phoenician syllabary.

Modern Hebrew and modern Arabic scripts developed from the ancient Semitic writing system, which was of the syllabic type. The Hebrew and the Arabic alphabets seem to resemble each other, but their individual letters are quite different. Compare, for example, the first three letters of each alphabet:

Hebrew: א ב ג   Arabic: ا ب ت

In spite of the sometimes imperfect match between pronunciation and spelling, the graphic symbols of the syllabaries and the alphabets indicate the basic sounds of the language. Thus the symbols provide at least a partial clue to the speech mode of the language.

We recognize two basic sets of rules that govern writing: *caligraphy* and *orthography*. The first is concerned with the shapes of the symbols, the second with the spelling of words, that is, the proper order in which graphic symbols follow each other within a word.

Speech   Speaking is obviously the most frequent, efficient, and often the most effective mode of communication. It is the most important mode of communication in the order of our teaching priorities. The telephone, radio, television, and magnetic tape have increased the pragmatic importance of speech even for the literate half of the world's population. Writing, in the usual sense of the term, has never been known to exist without speech. Robert Hall, Jr. supports the claim for the primacy of speech by saying that "the spelling of a word is never more than a reflection (in English orthography, often a very imperfect reflection) of the way it is pronounced; changing the spelling of the word does not change the word itself...."[1] The fact is that native speakers do not mispronounce the words they often misspell.

The History of Speech   Prehistoric man, capable of thinking, sought primarily lingual means of communication with his fellow man. He had a voice able to produce a great variety of sounds with which to create some sort of speech. We do not exactly know how he went about it. Cultural anthropologists have not yet established an authoritative theory about the original stages of human speech. Some earlier students of the problem thought that man's lingual communication was originally not too much different from that of animals and birds. On one of the Canary Islands, the natives still use a language that consists of a variety of whistling sounds audible at long distance, and there are other societies that have a kind of whistled language, such as the Magatec of Mexico and a few African tribes. Present-day thinking, however, does not favor the theory that onomatopoetic expressions, such as "bow-wow," "coo," and the like, were at the basis of man's original speech sounds. Speech is a purely human and noninstinctive method of communicating ideas, emotions, and desires. It is an intricate system of voluntarily produced sounds. Just as drawing single letters does not constitute writing (a man painting Russian characters on a billboard is not necessarily writing Russian), so making human sounds, which certain birds can do, does not necessarily constitute speaking a language.

The Act of Speech   Speaking is not only a physiological but also a psychological process:

---

[1] Robert H. Hall, Jr., *Introductory Linguistics* (New York: Chilton Books, 1964), pp. 8–9.

"The action of speech begins with the psychological link that has been previously established in the speaker's mind between a given concept and the set of sounds used to symbolize it. But almost immediately a physiological process sets in. A nerve impulse sends out the command from the brain to the vocal organs to produce the sound sequence that it is desired to transmit. The vocal organs go into the physiological operation and produce the audible sound sequence which is transmitted by physical sound waves to the listener's ear. The ear, in turn, transmits the sounds it has received to the hearer's brain..."[1]

The production of a spoken message, the wording of a thought, is called *encoding*. The reception of the message, the comprehension of the speaker's thought, is called *decoding*.

These two processes, of which one is oral and the other aural, consist of three phases each:

1. Semantic,
2. Syntactic,
3. Phonological.

Semantic encoding involves a choice of concepts, a decision to say something with certain words.

Syntactic encoding is an arrangement in the speaker's mind of the chosen words according to a habitual and meaningful order.

Phonological encoding is the physical production of sounds (in the intended order) which form the acoustic image (words) of the chosen semantic concepts.

The acoustic images encoded by the speaker are transmitted to the ear of the listener. The agent of transmission is the air, or rather the acoustic air waves created by the speech sounds emitted in the air. When the sounds reach the ear, the three phases of decoding take place, but in reverse order.

Phonological decoding comes first. It involves the ear's filtering the sounds, converting them into nerve impulses and channeling them to the brain. The second and third phases are syntactic decoding and semantic decoding, respectively. The result of both is the conversion

---

[1] Pei, p. 7.

of the nerve impulses by the brain to meaningful concepts that are normally, but not necessarily, identical to those of the speaker.

Mutual comprehension is made possible by the presence of identical concepts in the brains of the speaker and the listener. The matching of these concepts need not follow immediately the reception by the listener. Frequently, the latter's decoding lags behind the speaker's encoding. In order to decode well, the listener must sometimes wait until he has received a certain segment of the total message.

This ability to withhold an immediate decoding of every received word is a significant factor in listening comprehension. The beginning learner of a foreign language is apt to feel that he cannot wait until he has heard a sound sequence representing several words. Yet it is often only such a seemingly long sequence that reveals the proper meaning of the words within its first and its last sound. The beginner's listening-comprehension problem is similar to the problem he will have with reading. In reading we notice more readily how the beginner tends to decode prematurely (literally) each word as he sees it, instead of first visually registering all the segments of a phrase.

Language teachers are properly concerned with the problems of facilitating the student's decoding (listening) and encoding (speaking) in the new language. We should bear in mind the three phases of each process, while we recognize that all three are integrated, on the surface at least, into the familiar audio-lingual method.

In a later chapter relevant to decoding, we shall discuss a pragmatic approach to listening problems, based on audio-lingual drills. The encoding process can be pursued in the learning of vocabulary, syntax, and phonology. What follows immediately is intended to deepen our knowledge of the phonological phase of encoding.

PRODUCING SPEECH SOUNDS

Traditionally, speech sounds are considered the "building blocks" of a language. They are customarily divided into *vowels, consonants, semivowels* (or *semiconsonants*), and *diphthongs*. We can categorize them according to their acoustical properties. Different languages

have different basic speech sounds, varying from about thirty to
fifty. The proportion of vocalic sounds to consonantal sounds also
varies from language to language. English, French, and German are
richer in the variety of vowels than some other occidental languages.
There are eleven vocalic sounds in English, sixteen in French (including four nasals), fourteen in German, but only seven in Italian, seven
in Russian, five in Spanish, and three in Eskimo (A, I, U).[1]

Vowels   The vowels of most languages are produced in the oral
or the nasal cavity. The parts of the vocal apparatus principally
engaged in the production of vowels are the vocal cords (the phonation of practically all vocalic sounds starts in the glottis), the velum,
the palate, and the lips. The tongue and the teeth play relatively
minor roles in the phonation of vowels.

Consonants   The consonants are produced usually by the interference of the tongue, the teeth, and the lips, creating an obstacle for
the air stream. The obstacle effects either a closure or a constriction
of the air stream. The latter results in a friction noise, such as the
initial sound in *far* or *phone*.

Semivowels   The semivowels (or semiconsonants) are sounds
whose production is partly consonantal and partly vocalic, such as
in the initial sound of *wade* or *yoke*. The American English initial
sound in *radio*, as it is sometimes pronounced, belongs also in this
category.

Diphthongs   The diphthongs result from a quick transition in
producing one vowel to producing another vowel while the sound
(phonation) of the first vowel is still in progress; that is, in a diphthong we pronounce two sounds within the time it normally takes to
pronounce only one.[2]

Certain languages in South Africa contain rather queer speech
sounds referred to as clicks. These sounds are produced by forming

---

[1] Some dialects of English, French, and German have fewer vowels than
indicated here.
[2] A diphthong must be distinguished from a glide, which is normally an
accidental sound created by the passing of the vocal organs to or from a
position for the production of consonants.

little popping vacuums between the tongue and the roof of the oral cavity. An equally peculiar sound is the so-called glottal stop, the medial sound we hear in the Eastern American pronunciation of *bottle.*

Generally speaking, the sounds of most languages are produced by the stream of air leaving the lungs under a certain amount of pressure and passing through or by the various organs of speech. The figure below shows the location of these organs and of the equally important areas of resonance.

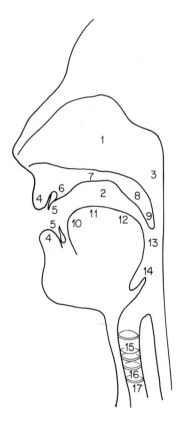

Vocal Tract

Location of Vocal Organs and Points of Reference in the Vocal Apparatus

1. Nasal cavity — area of resonance
2. Oral cavity — area of resonance
3. Nasal passage
4. Lips (labiae)
5. Teeth (dens)
6. Alveolar ridge
7. Hard palate
8. Velum (soft palate)
9. Uvula
10. Tip of the tongue (apex)
11. Middle of the tongue (lamina)
12. Back of the tongue (dorsum)
13. Pharynx — area of resonance
14. Epiglottis
15. Larynx
16. Vocal cords
17. Glottis

The primary organ where air from the lungs may be put to work to produce speech sounds is the larynx (Adams apple or voice box), which contains the vocal cords. The vocal cords are two elastic membranes (*ligamenta vocalica*) somewhat comparable to the lips. The space created by the opening of the vocal cords is called the glottis.

The following sketch of the larynx shows the vocal cords in closed and open position:

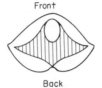

When we breathe without talking, our vocal cords are at rest and the glottis is fully open. When we produce certain consonantal sounds, such as those represented by B, D, G, Z, L, R, and all the vowel sounds, our vocal cords narrow or constrict the glottis and thus create an obstacle to the upsurging air. This air sets the cords in vibration, and the resulting sound, modulated by other parts of the vocal apparatus, becomes the desired speech sound. Any such sound produced with the cooperation of the vocal cords is called "voiced" or "cordal."

The speed at which the vocal cords vibrate, that is, the pitch of a person's voice, is partly contingent on age and sex. The vocal cords of women and children are thinner and shorter than those of adult men, whose voice is deeper because their vocal cords vibrate more slowly. The average vibration of vocal cords for men is 100–150 swings per second, whereas the average for women is from 200–300 per second. A low masculine voice represents 60–70 vibrations per second, and a soprano achieves from 1200–1300 swings per second. Depending on the frequency of vibration, the pitch of a person's voice (sound waves) is either high or low. The amplitude of vibrations, that is, how tightly the glottis is closed, determines the intensity of a person's voice. The tighter the glottis is closed for each vibration, the more intense is the sound and vice versa.

The sound-producing vibration of our vocal cords, however, is not necessary for all speech sounds. Those which are produced without the vocal cords, such as F, K, P, S, T, are called voiceless or unvoiced; they represent a minority among the speech sounds of the Western languages.

The other areas through which the air from the lungs passes, after leaving the glottis, are the pharynx (with the overhanging uvula), the nasal passage, the oral cavity (within the tongue, the cheeks, and the palate), the teeth, and the lips. All these parts of our throat and mouth have an important function in the production of speech sounds.

SYMBOLIZATION OF SPEECH SOUNDS

Phonetic Symbols   Since human vocal organs can produce an amazingly large number of vocalic and consonantal sounds, sharp classifications and complete charts would show an unmanageable number of phonetic symbols. For example, the following symbols can be used to distinguish among the various sounds which may appear acoustically the same to an average speaker of American English as the vowel in *bet*: [e], [ɛ], [ə], [œ], [ø], [ɜ]. (To indicate that these graphic symbols represent units of the sound system and not units of the writing system, the symbols are customarily placed between brackets [ ].)

Professor Higgins in G. B. Shaw's comedy *Pygmalion* (1900) apparently distinguishes one hundred and thirty symbols for distinct English vowel sounds, of which he tells his friend Colonel Pickering: "You hear no difference at first; but you keep on listening, and presently you find they are all as different as A and B."

Scientific procedure can indeed identify all kinds of sounds in the dialects of any language. Tomás Navarro proposed a twenty-vowel system for Spanish: four sounds for "i," three for "e," six for "a," three for "o," and four for "u."[1]

---

[1] Tomás Navarro, *Manuel de pronunciación española* (Madrid: R.F.E., 1932).

By means of special equipment, such as the spectrograph, phoneticians easily identify several variants of every vowel as well as of every consonant. In English, for example, we find three variants of the sound of "p." To mark the sound when it is accompanied by a strong aspiration (a puff of breath), which occurs in inital prevocalic position, we use a diacritic in the form of a raised ᴴ. Thus the word **pin** is phonetically transcribed [pᴴɪn]. When the aspiration is noticeable, but not very strong, we use a diacritic in the form of a raised ʰ; example: **peppy** [pᴴɛpʰɪ]. The German word **Papier** (paper) is transcribed [pʰapᴴiːʌ].

If a normally nonnasal sound takes on a little nasalization (a resonance in the nasal cavity), the phonetician refers to a "nasal release" and indicates it by a raised ᴺ. For example, the German **haben** (to have) and **baden** (to bathe) are transcribed [haːbᴺn] and [baːdᴺn].

Note that the lengthening of the vowel is marked by a colon, used as a diacritic after the vocalic symbol. This diacritic is sometimes used in English in the transcription of words like **beat** [biːt], **palm** [paːm], or **eel** [iːl]. In French the customary lengthening of vowels before certain consonants may also be indicated by this diacritic: **active** [aktiːv], **vers** [vɛːʀ], **la prise** [lapʀiːz] (the capture). Note that to distinguish between the sound of the English and the French r the phonetician uses the symbol [ʀ] for the French sound. For the Spanish sound he uses [ř].

The unvoiced French l as in **table** may be marked by a small circle under the symbol: [tabḷ]. In Russian the palatalization of consonants in certain positions is represented by a lowered comma: кислый [ķiːslɪj] (sour) or здесь [zḍeṣ] (here). In Castilian Spanish the palatalization of ll is also marked by this diacritic: **calle** [kaḷe] (street), **caballo** [kabaḷo] (horse).

The number of diacritics (raised or lowered commas, letters, dots, circles, and curves) used to indicate minor acoustic shades of difference is large. Moreover, phoneticians in different countries use different diacritics for the same phonetic phenomena.

The International Phonetic Alphabet   An international effort to standardize phonetic symbols and diacritics was undertaken by the Association Phonétique Internationale, to which we owe the International Phonetic Alphabet.[1] The IPA (a frequently-used abbreviation for the Alphabet) succeeded several other phonetic writing systems. It is intended for the representation of speech sounds in any and all of the known languages of the world. (Additions could be made if new sounds in any language were discovered.) The IPA shows a manageable number of basic phonetic symbols (82), but it has not sufficiently reduced the number of diacritics to facilitate teaching.

Phonemic Symbols For language learners and teachers, it is helpful to further simplify the phonetic symbols of sounds and to concentrate primarily on those that distinguish one word from another. This simplification need not be as crude as the "phonetic" notations in most dictionaries. Such notations are usually based on orthography supplemented by a variety of diacritic marks.

The sound notation which most teachers interested in functional linguistics prefer to use is a practical adaptation of the symbols of the IPA. It is, in fact, a selection of the functional sounds of French, German, Russian, and Spanish. The functional sounds are represented by symbols called phonemic symbols. Phonemics is a branch of phonetics dealing with the description of functional sounds involving *differences* between pairs of words in a given language, regardless of dialectal or other variations. As examples may serve the sounds **p** and **b** in English **pin** and **bin,** French **pompe** and **bombe,** German **packen** and **backen,** or Spanish **pollo** and **bollo.** It must be understood, of course, that each phonemic symbol represents a variety of phonetically different, but noncontrastive sounds of the language. Thus, English **p** and **b** are different on the phonetic level from French or German **p** and **b,** but they are considered the same on the phonemic level.

The Functional Phonemic Alphabet A system of phonemic symbols is called a phonemic alphabet. Apart from a few imita-

---

[1] The Association Phonétique publishes a semiannual journal, *Le maître phonétique,* with articles in English and other languages printed in the phonetic alphabet. The table on page 14 is reprinted by permission.

THE INTERNATIONAL PHONETIC ALPHABET.

(Revised to 1951.)

		Bi-labial	Labio-dental	Dental and Alveolar	Retroflex	Palato-alveolar	Alveolo-palatal	Palatal	Velar	Uvular	Pharyngal	Glottal
CONSONANTS	Plosive	p b		t d	ʈ ɖ			c ɟ	k g	q ɢ		ʔ
	Nasal	m	ɱ	n	ɳ			ɲ	ŋ	ɴ		
	Lateral Fricative			ɬ ɮ								
	Lateral Non-fricative			l	ɭ			ʎ				
	Rolled			r						ʀ		
	Flapped			ɾ						ʀ		
	Fricative	ɸ β	f v	θ ð s z ʃ ʒ	ʂ ʐ	ʃ ʒ	ɕ ʑ	ç ʝ	x ɣ	χ ʁ	ħ ʕ	h ɦ
	Frictionless Continuants and Semi-vowels	w ɥ	ʋ	ɹ	ɻ			j (ɥ)	(w)	ʁ		

VOWELS		Front		Central		Back	
Close.		(y ʉ u) i y		ɨ ʉ		ɯ u	
Half-close.		(ø o)			ə		ɤ o
Half-open.		(œ ɔ) ɛ œ		œ	ɐ	ʌ ɔ	
Open.		(ɒ)		æ	a	ɑ ɒ	

(Secondary articulations are shown by symbols in brackets.)

OTHER SOUNDS.—Palatalized consonants : ʧ, ɖ, etc.; palatalized ʃ, ʒ : ꞔ, ꭦ. Velarized or pharyngalized consonants : ɫ, ɖ, z, etc. Ejective consonants (with simultaneous glottal stop): p', t', etc. Implosive voiced consonants : ɓ, ɗ, etc. ʀ fricative trill. σ, ϩ (labialized θ, ð, or s, z). ɮ, ʒ (labialized ʃ, ʒ). ɬ, ʟ, ƫ, ʗ, ʖ (clicks, Zulu c, q, x). l (a sound between r and l). ŋ Japanese syllabic nasal. ʄ (combination of x and ʃ). ʍ (voiceless w). ɩ, ʏ, ɵ (lowered varieties of i, y, u). ɜ (a variety of ə). ɵ (a vowel between ø and o).

Affricates are normally represented by groups of two consonants (ts, tʃ, dʒ, etc.), but, when necessary, ligatures are used (ʦ, ʧ, ʤ, etc.), or the marks ͡ or ͜ (ts or ts, etc.). ͜ also denote synchronic articulation (m͡ŋ = simultaneous m and ŋ). c, ɟ may occasionally be used in place of tʃ, dʒ, and ʃ, ʒ for ts, dz. Aspirated plosives : ph, th, etc. r-coloured vowels : eɹ, aɹ, ɔɹ, etc., or eˑ, aˑ, ɔˑ, etc., or ə, ɐ, etc.; r-coloured ə : əɹ or əˑ or ɹ or ɚ.

LENGTH, STRESS, PITCH.—ː (full length). ˑ (half length). ˈ (stress, placed at beginning of the stressed syllable). ˌ (secondary stress). ˉ (high level pitch); ˍ (low level); ˊ (high rising); ˏ (low rising); ˋ (high falling); ˎ (low falling); ˆ (rise-fall); ˇ (fall-rise).

MODIFIERS.—˜ nasality. ̥ breath (l̥ = breathed l). ˬ voice (ʂ = z). ˈ slight aspiration following p, t, etc. ˴ labialization (n̫ = labialized n). ̩ dental articulation (t̪ = dental t). ˴ palatalization (z̩ = ʒ). ˴ specially close vowel (e̩ = a very close e). ˴ specially open vowel (e̜ = a rather open e). ̝ tongue raised (e̝ or e̝ = e̝). ̞ tongue lowered (e̞ or e̞ = e̞). ̟ tongue advanced (u̟ or u = an advanced u, t̟ = t̟). ̠ or ̠ tongue retracted (i̠ or i = ɨ, t̠ = alveolar t). ̣ lips more rounded. ̣ lips more spread. Central vowels : ɨ (= i̠), ʉ (= u̟), ə̈ (= ə̈), ɵ (= o̝), ɛ̈, ɔ̈, (e.g. n̩) syllabic consonant. ̯ consonantal vowel. ʃ variety of ʃ resembling s, etc.

tions of Greek letters, the majority of the symbols of the phonemic alphabet are lower-case letters of the standard typewriter, using the Latin alphabet. This practical choice of phonemic symbols necessitates the use of near-vertical lines or slashes to indicate that the symbols within the slashes represent sounds that are often different from the way we pronounce individual letters of our alphabet. For example, the slashes around the symbol /a/ indicate that it represents the vowel sound in American-English **odd, pot, spot,** which are phonemically transcribed /ad/, /pat/, /spat/. We must not confuse the Latin alphabet with the symbols of the sound system.

Languages using other than Latin letter symbols (for example, Russian, Hebrew, and Arabic) can be transcribed without the problem of confusion between phonemic symbols and letters of the respective systems of writing. The sound symbols are, of course, indispensable in the transcription of languages which have no writing system.

Duplicity of Symbols   Ideally, one symbol of the phonemic alphabet should represent consistently only one functionally significant sound of the language in question. In practice, we find that more than one phonemic symbol may be used for the transcription of functionally identical sounds. Some descriptive linguists interpret the **ea** of **beat** or the **ie** of **field** as two compressed sounds (a diphthong) and use in addition to the symbol /i/ another symbol, which may be either /ɪ/, /y/, or /j/. The transcription of **beat** may then be either /bit/, /bɪt/, /biyt/, or /bijt/. Some consider the vowels in **palm** and **saw** as types of diphthongs and transcribe them /ah/ and /ɔh/, respectively (see Paul Roberts). Others stress quantity and indicate the lengthening of a vowel neither by adding /h/ nor by using a colon as a diacritic, but by doubling the symbol. Thus **beat** may be found transcribed as /biit/ and **palm** as /paam/ (see Henry Sweet).

Single speech sounds represented by two letters (called a digraph), such as **sh** in **ship,** are transcribed by a single phonemic symbol, which may be either /ʃ/ or /š/ for the initial sound in **ship.** Sounds such as the initial consonants in **chip** and **Jim** are sometimes considered simple sounds and are represented by the symbols /č/ and /ǰ/, respectively. Some linguists feel, however, that there are two sounds involved and prefer to use the symbols /tš/ or /tʃ/ in transcribing **ch** of **chip** and either /dž/ or /dǰ/ in transcribing J in **Jim**. We must simply accept the fact that descriptive linguists have not yet completely agreed about representing identical sounds by the same symbols.

There is also a lack of agreement about the number of relevant sounds in the various languages. Some linguists claim that English has only nine vowels. Others find eleven or even twelve. The number depends on where one draws the boundaries between vowels and diphthongs.[1]

The table of sound symbols on pages 18-20 reflects the opinion of linguists who find a somewhat larger number of phonemically meaningful sounds than others do. Its purpose, however, is not to present an exact number of relevant sounds in English, French, German, Spanish, or Russian, but to show the symbols used to represent the sounds.

The International *Phonetic* Alphabet has obvious merits, but it has one disadvantage for us. It abounds in symbols and diacritics that are not on the keyboards of our typewriters; and most of them are not easy to write by hand. The *phonemic* alphabet, on the other hand, is functionally limited and unsuitable for comparative work in several languages. Its use presupposes that our students know the foreign language well enough to be aware of the variations within any sound we transcribe. In other words, the symbols of the purely phonemic alphabet do not show the differences between such sounds as the /r/ in English and in the foreign language, or the /b/ in **abolish** and in Spanish **abolir.**

Modified Phonemic Alphabet   Practicing teachers of one and often more than one commonly taught foreign language prefer a

---

[1] Robert L. Politzer, *Foreign Language Learning, A Linguistic Introduction* (Englewood Cliffs: Prentice-Hall, 1965) pp. 32–33, lists eleven vowels, but points out that /u/ as in **food** and /o/ as in **boat** are highly diphthongal. Robert Lado, *Language Teaching* (New York: McGraw-Hill, 1964) p. xiii, lists nine vowels and seven diphthongs, among which he includes the vowels in **beet** and **boat**.

modified phonemic transcription system in which the variations within certain sounds are clearly marked.

In the modified phonemic alphabet we employ phonetic symbols whenever the phonemic symbols would not sufficiently reveal significant acoustic differences between the sounds of two languages. Thus we use the symbol /ʀ/ for French r and the symbol /r̄/ for the trilled Spanish variant. The striking phonetic difference between the vowel in **bill** and in **был** (was) will be marked by transcribing the former with /ɪ/ and the latter with /ɨ/. We use the diacritic /:/ to express the difference between the French or Spanish **si**, transcribed /si/, and the English **sea** /si:/.

We also include the symbol /ɑ/ in addition to /a/: Not all English speakers contrast the vowels in **cot** and **cart**, yet in German and to some extent in French the contrast must not be ignored. We also introduce the symbol /o/ in addition to /ɔ/ as an English vowel symbol. (Some phoneticians claim that /o/ is not an English vowel but occurs only as the first sound of a diphthong in words like **open, boat**.) It helps us indicate that in words like **off, bore, core,** many speakers of English use a vowel quite comparable to the /o/ of a foreign language.[1]

Flexibility is the guiding principle in the use of the modified phonemic alphabet. Whenever there is no risk of confusing one sound with another, we can dispense with using symbols such as /ɑ/, /ɨ/, and the diacritics.

Table of Sound Symbols   The following table of sounds used in English, French, German, Russian, and Spanish gives all the symbols necessary for a meaningful phonemic transcription. (For a more detailed description of various foreign sound variants, see Chapter 6.)

For each phonemic symbol in the table, we list the letters (in bold type) representing the sound. All Russian words are transcribed in full to enable comparison of the sound in all five languages. The first

---

[1] See the use of /o/ in Van Nostrand's *Concise Student Dictionary*, prepared by the Lexicographic Research Center, University of Montreal (New York: Van Nostrand Reinhold, 1962).

symbol of each line is the one we use in our transcriptions. The second is given only to indicate that an alternate form of the symbol exists. The English, French, German, Spanish, and Russian words in the table contain sounds representing acceptable acoustic values of the symbols in the first column, although, in practice, there may be considerable acoustic variation from speaker to speaker.

Table of Sound Symbols

SYMBOLS	ENGLISH	FRENCH	GERMAN	SPANISH	RUSSIAN
VOWELS					
/i/		lit		cine	/bil/ бил
/i:/ /iy/	beat		sie		
/ɪ/	bit		sitzt		
/ɨ/					/bɪl/ был
/y/ /ü/		lune	süß		
/e/		les	sehen	se	/bek/ бег
/ø/ /ö/		l'œuf	Söhne		
/ɛ/	bet	l'herbe	sechs		
/æ/	bat				
/œ/ /ɔ̈/		leur	Löffel		
/ə/	beret	lever	sehe		/bánə/ баня
/ʌ/	but		Seher		/bʌrán/ баран
/a/	box	laver	satt	saber	/bánə/ баня
/ɑ/	bark	las	Saat		
/o/	bore	l'eau	so	sobre	/bok/ бок
/ɔ/	bought	l'os	soll		
/u/	boot	l'ours	suche	surdo	/búkvə/ буква
/ʊ/	book		Sucht		
/ɜ/ /ə:/	bird				
/ɛ̃/		linge			
/õ/ /ɔ̃/		long			
/ã/ /ɑ̃/		l'ange			
/œ̃/		un			

Table of Sound Symbols—Continued

SYMBOLS	ENGLISH	FRENCH	GERMAN	SPANISH	RUSSSAN
		SEMIVOWELS AND SEMICONSONANTS			
/h/	him		hin		
/j/ /y/	yes	fille	ja	hoy	/jizɪk/ язык
/w/	wine	ouest		hueso	
		CONSONANTS			
/b/	bad	bon	Berg	bueno	/bal/ бал
/ƀ/ /ß/				sabe	
/c/ /ts/	tse-tse		ziehe		/cɣet/ цвет
/č/ /tš/	batch			mucho	/čas/ час
/d/	do	donne	dann	deja	/dom/ дом
/đ/ /ð/	lather			lado	
/f/	fire	faire	Vater	fino	/funt/ фунт
/g/	good	gant	gut	gasa	/got/ год
/g/ /ɣ/				pagar	
/x/			Chemie	joven	/xot/ ход
/k/	king	car	Kamm	casa	/kot/ кот
/l/	long	langue	lang	ley	/láfkə/ лавка
/m/	my	moi	mehr	mas	/mak/ мак
/n/	nine	nous	nie	no	/nos/ нос
/ñ/	onion	agneau		año	
/ŋ/	sing		singen		
/p/	press	pour	Post	pase	/pakt/ пакт
/r/[1]	red				
/ř/ /ɼ/		recht		pero	/ruká/ рука
/rr/ /ɼ/				perro	
/R/		rire	Herr		
/s/	system	cent	essen	seco	/son/ сон
/š/ /ʃ/	ship	charme	Schiff		/šak/ шаг

[1] Sometimes a semivowel.

Table of Sound Symbols—Continued

SYMBOLS	ENGLISH	FRENCH	GERMAN	SPANISH	RUSSIAN
/t/	table	table	Tasse	teja	/tut/ тут
/v/	vine	va	weg		/vor/ вор
/ǰ/ /dž/	joke				
/θ/	thin			hace⎫ (Castilian pron.) hizo⎭	
/ž/ /ʒ/	measure	jour			/žal/ жал
/šč/					/ščit/ щит

DIPHTHONGS

/ej/ /ey/	bait			sabeis	
/aj/ /ay/	by		leider	aire	/maj/ май
/oj/ /oy/	boy		Leute	hoy	/moj/ мой
/uj/ /uy/	ruin			ouida	
/au/ /aw/	bowel		laut	causa	
/ou/ /ow/	bone				
/ju/	mute			ciudad	
/eu/				feudal	
/ua/		toi		cuadro	

(This list of diphthongs reflects the existing uncertainty as to the proper boundries between diphthongs, off-glides, and semivowels.)

Note that in our Table preference is given to symbols available on the standard keyboard of a typewriter, as in /š/ instead of /ʃ/ and /ž/ instead of /ʒ/. We also prefer single symbols over double symbols: /c/ over /ts/, etc. The reason for this preference is not only economy but also the belief that our symbols indicate better the coarticulation of what some phoneticians consider two sounds. In the symbol /rr/ we follow R. P. Stockwell's analysis of the Spanish trilled variant of /r/ and his reasons for the use of the double symbol.[1]

The Table does not include symbols of the palatalized consonant sounds of Russian, because of their rather large number. But it

[1] Robert P. Stockwell, *The Sounds of English and Spanish* (Chicago: U. of Chicago Press, 1965), pp. 49–50.

includes /č/ and /šč/, since they symbolize sounds which cannot be other than palatalized.

Other Russian consonant sounds, except /c/, /š/, /ž/, have a palatalized functional counterpart or variant. These variants are symbolized by a diacritic added to the primary symbol. The diacritic may be a raised comma, a raised "soft sign" of the Russian alphabet (/ᵇ/), or, preferably, a lowered comma. Here are a few examples of the phonemic transcription of palatalized consonants: /b̦élɨj/ (white), /r̦eká/ (river), /braț/ (to take), /ɣeș/ (all). More information is given in later chapters of this book.

READING AND WRITING PRACTICE

Using the words given below, let us now do the following:

1. Cover the second column on the page.

2. Read the English words in the first column. Check the second column only if you have to.

3. Uncover the second column and cover the first column.

4. Using our symbols in the Table, provide a modified phonemic transcription for each word in the second column. (Use space between the first [covered] and the second column.)

5. Check your transcriptions against those of the first column.

6. Procede in the same manner with at least one of the foreign word series.

sɪŋ	sing	fu	fou
sɪt	sit	fø	feu
si:t	seat	fəzɛ	faisais
sɛl	sell	fyme	fumé
sejv	save	fot	faute
skul	school	œʀ	heure
skʌl	scull	dã	dans
skɑr	scar	dɛ̃d	dinde
skær	scare	žuʀ	jour
mʌst	must		
moust	most	dɛʀse	der See

bas	boss	mɛtxən	Mädchen
bojz	boys	šøn	schön
ǰɛm	gem	ybuŋ	Übung
læŋwɪǰ	language	bux	Buch
laud	loud	ce:n	zehn
lɔd	laud	dɔjčə	Deutsche
əl	all		
bɜd	bird	asta	hasta
i:θɜ	ether	bjexo	viejo
i:ʤɜ	either	rrosa	rosa
mɪšn	mission	bebeř	bever
vɪžn	vision	adonde	adonde
čɜč	church	weřta	huerta
ǰʌǰ	judge	desiř	decir
ənʌf	enough	xugař	jugar
juənaj	you and I	kařne	carne
kouapərejt	cooperate	sweřte	suerte
bi:ŋ	being		
stɜ	stir	m̦il	мнл
ajhæv	I have	mɨl	мыл
dəmakrəsɪ	democracy	ţiátr	театр
ʌnbɪli:vɪŋ	unbelieving	am̦iɽikán̦ic	американец
lɪtərəčɜ	literature	fṣigdá	всегда
		tóžə	тоже

Now read the following transcription in which some conventional
spacing has been allowed for easier reading:

tədej moustəmɛrɪkənskulz hæv læŋgwiǰlæbərətɔrɪz

ožuʀdwi ilja de laboratwɑʀdəlãg dã laplupaʀ dezekɔlzameʀikẽn
(Aujourd'hui, il y a des laboratoires de langue dans la plupart
   des écoles américaines.)

hɔjtə giptɛs špraxlaboratorjən indenmajstən amɛrikanišənšulən
(Heute gibt es Sprachlaboratorien in den meisten amerikani-
   schen Schulen.)

ojdia aj laboratoriosdelengwa enlamajorparte delaseskẃelas
   amerikanas
(Hoy día hay laboratorios de lengua en la major parte de las
   escuelas americanas.)

șivodņa vbaļšinstye aṃiŗikansķix škol iṃejuca ļingyisțičiskijǝ
laboratóŗii
(Сегодня в большинстве американских школ имеются
лингвистические лаборатории.)
The rather difficult symbols to learn are /y/ and /ø/ in French and
in German and /x/ in German, Russian, and Spanish. The symbols
asked for in the following exercise may also seem unusual.

Write down the phonemic symbols for the last two sounds in each of
these words:

breath	bathe	hatch	barge	hush	rose
beige	hat	sing	bang	nation	visor

Answers:

/εθ/	/ejđ/	/æč/	/ɑj/	/ʌš/	/ouz/
/ejž/	/æt/	/ɪŋ/	/æŋ/	/šn/	/zɜ/

CLASSIFICATION OF SPEECH SOUNDS

Consonant Sounds   Distinctions between various sounds are
caused by *voicing* or *unvoicing* the air stream in the glottis and by the
modification of the air stream effected by the lips or the tongue in a
certain manner and at certain points in the oral cavity. The function
of the lips and the tongue is not only to modify but also to stop the
sound-bearing airstream and divide it into meaningful units. Such
partial or complete obstruction of the airstream is called articulation,
and the lips and the tongue are called flexible articulators.

Points of Articulation   The points or areas of the constriction
or of the stopping of air (articulation) by the flexible articulators are
called points of articulation. (See Table of Consonant Sounds, page
27.)

The names given to the various points of articulation are derived
from their location in the vocal tract (see the figure on page 9).
When the articulation is effected by a partial or a complete closure of
the lips, we say that the sound has a labial or bilabial point of articulation. When the upper or the lower front teeth are part of the

obstacle presented to the airstream, we speak of a dental point of articulation. The tongue, as articulator, can assume many positions and modify the sound production in several ways. Depending on what part of the tongue is effecting the constriction of air, we distinguish these points: *apical, laminal* (frontal and central), and *dorsal.* The rigid part of the oral cavity, the palate, can be similarly divided into the following points: *alveolar, palatal,* and *velar.* For certain sounds the tongue moves to the uvula. In some languages, such as Arabic, the pharynx is also an area of air constriction and we speak of a pharyngeal point of articulation.

Manner of Articulation   In addition to their particular points of articulation, speech sounds are also classified according to manner of articulation. To classify a given speech sound, it is customary to add to the name of the point of articulation a word which is descriptive of the manner of articulation. (See Table of Consonant Sounds, page 27.)

Stops   If the articulators stop the airstream completely and sound is produced by a sudden release (sometimes a plosion) of the air, such as in the initial sounds of **pit, bit, tip, dig, kid, gift,** we categorize the sound as a *stop* or *occlusive* (the term *plosive* is also used). Thus /p/ is an unvoiced sound articulated by the closure of the lips, which stops the airstream; hence, /p/ has a bilabial point of articulation and is called a bilabial unvoiced stop. /b/ is a bilabial voiced stop. /t/ is articulated by the tip (apex) of the tongue touching the alveolar ridge. It has an apico-alveolar point of articulation and is called an apico-alveolar unvoiced stop. /d/ has the same point of articulation but is voiced. It is therefore an apico-alveolar voiced stop. /k/ and /g/ are articulated by the stopping of the airstream between the back of the tongue and velum. They are dorso-velar stops. The first is unvoiced, the second is voiced.

Fricatives   If the obstacle does not completely stop the airstream and a sound is produced by the escaping air, such as in the initial sounds of **phone, think, sink, ship,** we categorize it as a *fricative* or *spirant.* /f/ is an unvoiced sound articulated by the lower lip touching the upper teeth. It is a labio-dental unvoiced fricative. The sound of /s/, articulated by the tip of the tongue (apex) in very loose contact with the alveolar ridge, is an apico-alveolar unvoiced fricative. (Because of its hissing quality, which distinguishes it from other fricatives, it is sometimes called a sibilant.) The sound of /θ/, as in **thin,** is articulated by placing the tip of the tongue between the teeth or in loose contact with the back of the teeth. It is an apico-interdental or apico-dental unvoiced fricative. The sound of /š/, as in *ship*, is articulated at the point of maximum constriction of air by the lamina of the tongue raised against the palate. It is therefore a lamino-palatal, unvoiced fricative. (Distinguish between *palatal* and *palatalized*. The latter term means that certain consonants are articulated with the tongue moved somewhat toward the palate, as for the initial sound in **you.**) The voiced counterparts of /t/, /s/, /θ/, /š/ are /d/, /z/, /đ/, /ž/. They are articulated at the same points and by the same manner of articulation, but their production requires the vibration of the vocal cords. The voiced sounds are sometimes called *cordals* or *sonorants*.

Three fricatives that do not exist in the English sound system are /ƀ/, /x/ and /g̶/. The first represents Spanish **b** or **v** in certain positions. It is produced by the air passing through the barely opened lips and is a bilabial voiced fricative. The second represents the final sound in German **Bach** /bax/ (brook), Russian **Воздух** /vózdux/ (air), or Spanish **reloj** /řelox/ (clock). This sound is articulated by raising the dorsum of the tongue so that it is in loose contact with the uvula. It is a uvular or velar unvoiced fricative. The third sound, /g̶/, is the voiced counterpart of /x/. It represents Spanish **g** between two vowels, the second of which is /a/, /o/, /u/ in such words as **pagar** (pay), **jugo** /xug̶o/ (juice), or **agua** /ag̶wa/ (water). It is a dorso-uvular voiced fricative. This sound should not be confused with English /h/ as in **hill,** which is articulated in the glottis and usually classified as an unvoiced glottal fricative or a semivowel. (Some phonemic transcriptions use the symbol /h/ for both the Spanish and the English sounds. Such use obscures the acoustic difference between the sounds.)

Affricates   If the closure and release of the air in the production of a sound is very rapid, such as in the initial sound of **chin** or **gin,** such sounds are called *affricates*. Because of their point of articulation (the lamina of the tongue touching the alveolar ridge), /č/ and /ǰ/ are lamino-alveolar affricates. The first is unvoiced, the second voiced.

Stops, fricatives, and affricates are collectively called *obstruants*.

Resonants   Several voiced consonants are collectively categorized as *resonants*. They are described according to their manner of articulation as lateral, retroflex, tapped, trilled, and nasal. Thus, because of its alveolar point of articulation, English /l/, the first sound in **law,** is an apico-alveolar lateral. Russian or Castilian /ļ/, the palatalized varient, is a lamino-alveolar lateral. English /r/, as in **red,** is an apico-alveolar retroflex, usually produced without an actual contact between the apex and the alveolar ridge. Russian and sometimes Spanish /ř/, as in **cara,** is an apico-alveolar tap. The typical Spanish /rr/ and the preferred French /ʀ/ are an apico-alveolar and a dorso-uvular trill, respectively. The German equivalent may be either an apico-alveolar tap /ř/ or a dorso-velar trill, symbolized /ʀ/.

Nasals are resonants for which the sound carrying air passes through the nasal cavity. Their points of articulation may be labial (/m/), apico-alveolar (/n/), lamino-palatal (/ñ/), or dorso-velar (/ŋ/).

Semiconsonants   Certain consonant sounds are produced by an incomplete suppression of any one of the articulatory obstructions to the flow of air in the oral cavity. Such sounds, as we said before, are classified as semiconsonants or semivowels. According to their point of articulation, they may be labial (/w/), lamino-alveolar (/j/), or glottal (/h/).

The classification of functional consonant speech sounds in English, French, Russian, and Spanish is presented in the following Table. Generally speaking, the points of articulation, listed horizontally, indicate where the sound is formed. The manner of articulation, listed vertically, indicates in what manner the stream of air is modified. The Table shows, for example, that /p/, /t/, and /k/ share the same manner of articulation, but each is articulated at a different point. The terms *apico, lamino,* and *dorso* refer to the tip, the middle, and the back of the tongue, respectively. Consonants articulated by either of the three parts of the tongue have two basic variants. For example, /t/ may be apico-dental, as in French, or apico-alveolar, as usually in English. This is why the horizontal heading indicates *dental* or *alveolar, alveolar* or *palatal*, etc.[1]

Consonant Sounds

	Points of Articulation						
Manner of Articulation	Bila-bial	Labio dental	Apico		Lamino alveo-lar or palatal	Dorso velar or uvular	Glottal
			dental or inter-dental	dental or alveo-lar			
Unvoiced ⎱ Stops	p			t	ṭ	k	
Voiced ⎰	b			d	ḍ	g	obstruants
Unvoiced ⎱ Fricatives		f	θ	s*	š	x	obstruants
Voiced ⎰	ƀ	v	đ	z*	ž	g	obstruants
Unvoiced ⎱ Affricates				c		č	obstruants
Voiced ⎰						ǰ	obstruants
Lateral				l		ļ	
Retroflex					r		resonants
Tapped					ř	ṛ	resonants
Trilled					rr		R resonants
Nasal	m				n	ñ ŋ	
Semiconsonants or Semivowels	w					j	h

* The sounds /s/ and /z/ are apico-dental, not alveolar, in English, French German, and Spanish.

Vocalic Sounds Vocalic sounds may be described, according to their point of articulation, as *front, central,* or *back,* depending on which part of the tongue is slightly raised and on which section of the oral cavity the turbulence in the stream of air is effected. They

[1] A more precise and elaborate classification of speech sounds is offered by the table of the IPA and other tables designed by researchers in phonetics. See Jacobson, Fant, & Halle, *Preliminaries to Speech Analysis* (M.I.T. Press, 1952) and any of the more recent studies by Morris Halle. We prefer to present this broader, simpler, and more applicable Table.

also may be classified as *rounded* or *unrounded*, according to the position of the lips at the moment of articulation. Depending on their area of resonance, certain vowels are either oral or nasal.

The size of the opening (aperture) of the oral cavity may be another criterion for classification. It may be *narrow, half-open,* or *open.*

For practical purposes in connection with the following Table of Vocalic Sounds, the term *narrow* is synonymous with *high, half-open* with *middle,* and *open* with *low.* Raising the tongue is almost automatically accompanied by a narrowing or a decrease in the size of the air passage, and lowering the tongue by an increase in the air passage and in the opening of the lips. Thus the differences in articulating the vowels in **hoot, heart,** and **heat** are essentially threefold:

1. The point of turbulence on the roof of the oral cavity is moving from the velum to the alveolar ridge, so that /u/ is articulated in back and /i:/ in front.
2. The lips change considerably from the rounded position in phonating /u/ to the unrounded position in phonating /i:/.
3. The oral cavity increases for /ɑ/ in **heart** by a retraction of the tongue.

The three vowels are described as follows: /u/ in **hoot** is a back rounded, high vowel; /ɑ/ in **heart** is a central, low vowel; /i:/ in **heat** is a front, high vowel.

These descriptions can be refined by differentiating between higher, mean, and lower strata of the *high, mid,* and *low* areas. /æ/ in **hat** is then described as a front low-higher vowel, the /a/ in **hot** as a front low-lower vowel, and /ɛ/ of **hen** is a front mid-lower vowel.

The Table below indicates schematically the area of the oral cavity from the lips to the pharynx wall (horizontal listing), as well as the points within the clearance between the tongue and the roof of the oral cavity (vertical column), at which the various vowels are formed. It shows, for example, that /i/, /ɛ/, and /æ/ share the front area of the cavity, but have their point of articulation at different levels of the vertical scale. The vertical scale, divided into high, mid, and low levels, is subdivided to achieve a more accurate description. Nasalized vowels are marked with the diacritic /~/ placed over the vocalic symbol.

Vocalic Sounds

		FRONT	CENTRAL rounded	BACK ¡rounded
HIGH	higher	i i:	y	u
HIGH	lower	I		ɪ ᵕ
MID	higher	e	ø	o õ
MID	mean		ə ɜ ʌ	
MID	lower	ɛ ɛ̃	œ (œ̃)	ɔ
LOW	higher	æ		
LOW	lower	a ã	ɑ	

Another conventional way of illustrating the division into spatial segments of the oral cavity is the quadrilateral shown below. This, too, is a highly schematic illustration, but it at least accounts for the approximate profile of the cavity and for the fact that the jaw is movable and hinged at the back of the mouth. It also shows that the area available for the articulation of the front and central vowels is physiologically more expandable than the area for the back vowels.

Vocalic Quadrilateral

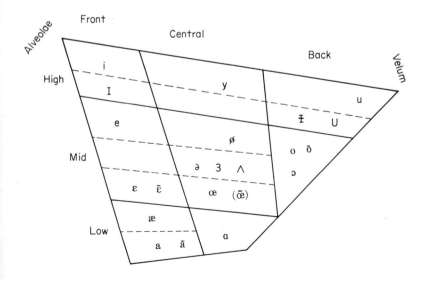

Learning Exercises

Pronounce twice, out loud, each of the words below. Try to feel and identify the area of maximum constriction between the articulators. For example, when you say *vice*, you feel your upper teeth touching your lower lip during the articulation of the first sound. Then you know that /v/ has a labio-dental point of articulation.

A. Determine the point of articulation of each first sound in these words. (Check your answers against the Table of Consonant Sounds. Do not let orthography mislead you.):

1. pet, bed, met, wet
2. fig, vice, phone
3. thin, then, tsetse
4. tomb, doom, zoom, room

5. ship, chip, jib, yes
6. kit, get, can, grab
7. hang, hot

B. Determine the point of articulation for each *final* sound in these words:

1. dam, tab, dip
2. deaf, have, laugh
3. both, bathe, Hertz

4. piece, peel, pin, pet
5. beige, batch, dash, ridge
6. bang, Buch (book)

C. Determine whether the first sound in each of the words below is voiced or unvoiced. As you say each word out loud, touch your Adam's apple (formed by the large cartilage of the larynx) with your thumb and forefinger. Only voiced sounds, for example, /b/ or /d/, should cause the "apple" to move:

1. bed, pet, fell, vine
2. tap, dad, sat, zoom

3. ship, gym, cat, gab
4. thin, than, tzar, church

ANSWERS: 1. v., unv., unv., v.
          2. unv., v., unv., v.
          3. unv., v., unv., v.
          4. unv., v., unv., unv.

D. Determine the manner of articulation of the first sound in each of the words in exercise C:

EXAMPLES: bed /b/ a stop, fell /f/ a fricative, etc.

Continue with the first sound of the following words:

lap, river, man, name, wine, yes, high, hang

E. Give complete phonemic descriptions (determine both the point and the manner of articulation) of the first sound in each of the words in exercises C and D:

> EXAMPLES: dam /d/ apico-alveolar voiced stop
> chin /č/ lamino-alveolar unvoiced affricate
> mat /m/ bilabial nasal

Check your answers against the Table of Consonant Sounds. Check also the complete description of /z/, /x/, /g/, /ƀ/, and /rr/.

F. Using the Table of Vocalic Sounds as a guide, give complete descriptions of the vowels in each of the following words:

beat, bit, bet, bat, box, bark, bought, boot, book, but

> MODEL ANSWERS: beat /i:/ a front high-higher vowel
> but /ʌ/ a central mid-mean vowel

Similarly, give the descriptions of the following foreign vocalic sounds: /y/,/ɨ/, /ø/, /õ/, /ã/, /œ/.

Review Questions

1. Which are the three general modes of communication?

2. What do we call the sciences dealing with the study of gestures or facial expressions?

3. What are the two general writing systems?

4. Which people use a writing system in which the graphic symbols are not indicative of the sounds of the language?

5. Which other alphabets exist besides the Latin alphabet?

6. Which two rules govern the system of alphabetic writing?

7. What do linguists call such expressions as "bow-wow," "coo," "splash," "crack," etc.?

8. What do linguists call the wording of a thought and what do they call the comprehension of spoken words?

9. Into what three phases (in logical order) may be divided the processes of speaking and listening referred to in 8?

10. Into what four categories are speech sounds traditionally divided?

11. In the production of what category of sounds does the tongue play only a minor role?

12. What organ of speech plays a major role in the production of the sub-category of sounds referred to as voiced?

13. a. As the stream of air passes outward from the lungs, the first place where it can be utilized for sound production is called the _____.

   b. The two shelves of tissue contained therein are called the

   _____.

   c. The space between these two shelves of tissue is called the

   _____.

   d. Next, the air reaches the space between the tongue and the back wall of the throat. This space is called the _____
   _____.

   e. At the top of this space is the back (soft) palate, also called the _____.

   f. The small flexible "icicle" which hangs from the back edge of the soft palate is called the _____

   _____.

14. Which are the phonetic diacritics often used for
   a. strong aspiration;
   b. normal aspiration;
   c. lengthening of vowels;
   d. palatalization of consonants?

15. What is the International Phonetic Alphabet?

16. Who is responsible for the creation and updating of the IPA?

17. How many basic symbols does the IPA have (revised to 1951)?

18. What types of sounds does a phonemic alphabet represent?

19. Phonemic differences are determined by
    a. voicing or unvoicing;
    b. manner of articulation;
    c. _____.

20. With reference to 19, give four voiced and four unvoiced sounds.

21. What other terms besides "stops" are used to describe manner of articulation?

22. What other terms besides "bilabials" are used to describe points of articulation?

23. Transcribe phonemically the following words:

breath	key
think	people
breathe	gym
this	it
chin	play
reach	great
general	vessel
bridge	bat
she	soup
wash	news
treasure	could
beige	boat
yes	slow
song	taught
democracy	cloth

Supplementary Reading

FRENCH

Albert Valdman, *Applied Linguistics — French* (New York: D. C. Heath, 1961), pp. 91–110.

Robert L. Politzer, *Teaching French* (Boston: Blaisdell, 1965). pp. 51–69.

GERMAN

William G. Moulton, *The Sounds of English and German* (Chicago: The U. of Chicago Press, 1962), pp. 21–25, 60–70.

RUSSIAN

Gunnard Fant, *Acoustic Theory of Speech Production* (S-Gravenhage: Mouton, 1960). Read eclectically the descriptions and analyses of contemporary Russian sounds.

SPANISH

Robert P. Stockwell and J. Donald Bowen, *The Sounds of English and Spanish* (Chicago: The U. of Chicago Press; 1965), pp. 35–43 and 116–119.

2 ARTICULATORY ECONOMY

THE FLUX OF LANGUAGE

Over a span of time, words in any language change pronunciation as well as meaning. The majority of words in present-day English, French, German, Russian, and Spanish evolved phonologically from those of a language spoken in several variants by a seminomadic people whose tribes populated eastern Europe and western Asia some five thousand years ago. With the spread of these tribes into new territories and with the passage of time, the small differences in the dialects of the separated groups became greater and greater. Probably as early as 2000 B.C., several distinct branches of the original language, commonly called Proto Indo-European, may have existed. We can identify these branches broadly as Germanic, Celtic, Italic (which includes Latin), Hellenic, Balto-Slavic, Armenian, and Indo-Iranian. The growth of each branch depended on many factors that were also responsible for a great deal of phonological change and crosspollination. William D. Whitney, of Yale University, put the fact of constant change in the speech habits of any nation as follows:

> It matters not to what part of the world we may go: if we find for any existing speech a record of its predecessor at some time distant from it in the past, we shall perceive that the two are different, mainly in proportion to the distance in time that separates them ... An English speaker even only of a century ago would find not a little in our every-day speech which he would understand with difficulty, or not at all; if we were to hear Shakespeare read aloud a scene from one of his own works, it would be in no small part unintelligible. ... Chaucer's English (500 years ago) we master by dint of good solid application and with considerable help from a glossary; and King Alfred's Eng-

lish (1000 years ago), which we call Anglo-Saxon, is not easier to us than German. All this, in spite of the fact that no one has gone about of set purpose to alter English speech, in any generation . . . any more than in our own.[1]

Without tracing too far the pronunciation of words like **three** and **ten** (German **drei** and **zehn**) to the Saxon **thrie** and **tehan,** or **eye** (German **Auge**) to the Old English **eage,** we can observe significant changes within the few centuries of Modern English. Seventeenth century poets like Pope and John Milton regularly rhymed **home** with **from,** and as early as the time of our grandfathers it was common in many areas to rhyme **sergeant** with **serpent** or **servant.** Looking at the Italic branch of Indo-European, we note such developments as shown in the following simple examples: **The father and the son are dead** in the seventh century Vulgar Latin was: **Illi pater et illi filius sunt morti.** In twelfth-century Old French it was: **Li pedre et li filz sunt mort.** In twentieth-century French the same sentence is: **Le père et le fils sont morts.** The modern language we speak is the youngest and still growing branch of a tree of languages which grew rather unevenly throughout human history. (See the diagram, "Family Tree of Languages," page 37.)

Our purpose here is to observe and analyze contemporary developments toward articulatory economy in the everyday language of native speakers. Some of our observations risk being unscientific, but they will not fail to be interesting for language teachers and students. The general articulatory economy phenomena brought to light in the following discussion will be illustrated by ready examples from English and from foreign languages. The discussion will be limited to phenomena representing the kind of articulatory economy obvious in the common pronunciation of, for example, **what are you doing** as /whatəjəduɪn/ or /whačəduɪn/.

There is something to be learned from a comparison of the working and of the appearances of a given phenomenon in our several languages. For this reason all Russian examples are given in transliteration, which is likely to make reading and comparisons easier. (The transliteration follows the system used by the Library of Congress.)

[1] William D. Whitney, *Life and Growth of Language: An Outline of Linguistic Science* (New York: Scribner & Co., 1875), pp. 33–34.

Schematic (Highly Simplified)
"Family Tree of Languages"
Showing the Relations of Most Indo-European Languages

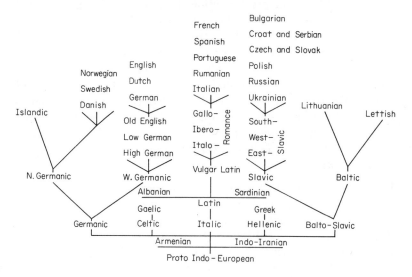

TENDENCY TO ECONOMIZE

Natural speakers of a language have an unconscious desire to express themselves with minimum articulatory effort. For this reason, their putting together the chain of sounds called speech tends to eliminate unessential articulatory movements. When they talk, they can afford many short cuts in the phonological code of the language, particularly when the topic is familiar to all. The goal of our advanced student must be to become aware of the tendencies toward economy in articulation in his language. Such awareness will facilitate his comprehension of the uninhibited speech of native speakers.

In present-day English, called Late Modern, we observe a tendency toward the so-called centralization (or gradation) of unstressed vowels. Centralization means moving the point of articulation toward the center of the oral cavity, that is, the area of the sounds symbolized /ə/. Notice that we pronounce **to separate** as /sepərejt/

and **it is separate** as /sɛprət/. The former is trisyllabic, the latter only twosyllabic. The latter exemplifies articulatory economy.

Similar tendencies in pronunciation have brought about the phonological and subsequently the occasional orthographic simplification of many words. In Middle English a final **e** was pronounced /ə/. Today it is completely lost in pronunciation and sometimes in spelling. Twosyllabic Middle English words like **oxe** /ɔksə/, **fode** /fɔdə/, **olde** /oldə/, became monosyllabic **ox** /ɔks/, **food** /fud/, and **old** /ould/. The trend toward monosyllables was carried even further in French. French has a silent **e** in final position, and a majority of final consonants (except where they occurred immediately before a vowel or at the end of a word cluster) ceased to be pronounced some three hundred years ago.[1]

The tendency toward silent **e** in final or in certain interconsonantal positions is noticeable today in colloquial German: **ich habe** /ixhabə/ (I have) may be pronounced /ixhap/. Words such as **Handel** (commerce), **schlagen** (to beat), **behandeln** (to discuss) are usually pronounced /handl/, /šlagn/, and /behandln/, respectively. (Note that the silencing occurs only in the last unstressed syllable in **behandeln.**)

A number of such contemporary tendencies toward articulatory economy will now be illustrated under special subheadings. Occasionally, our illustration of a phenomenon will refer to a tendency that may be observed mainly among uneducated people.

Dislocation of the primary point of articulation and of the primary manner of articulation   (See Table of Consonant Sounds in Chapter 1) This phenomenon is also known as phonetic variation caused by phonemic environment.

Unless they are uttered as isolated sounds, it is easier to articulate the consonants /d/, /t/, /g/, and /k/ at a point slightly closer to the

---

[1] The modern pronunciation of certain French numerals is a reminder of the earlier usage of final consonants: **Il a dix** /di/ **livres,** but **il en a dix** /diz/. Note that Spanish did not develop as many monosyllables as French: **champ** /šã/ is Spanish **campo** /kampo/ (field); **bras** /bra/ is Spanish **brazo** /brazo/ (arm); **vingt** /vẽ/ is Spanish **veinte** /bejnte/ (twenty); **quand** /kã/ is Spanish **cuando** /kwando/ (when).

point where the immediately following vowel or semivowel is articulated. For example, the articulation of /d/ in **dip** is apico-alveaolar, but the /d/ in **do** is almost apico-palatal. Similarly, the articulation of /g/ in **gear** is dorso-palatal, but the articulation of /g/ in **good** is dorso-velar or even dorso-uvular. With /h/, the point of articulation can in fact move between the glottal area and the alveolar ridge, depending on the vowel which follows; thus /h/ in **him** and **hooligan** or in **prohibit** and **courthouse.**

These examples make us aware that consonant sounds have certain secondary articulatory characteristics due to vocalic surroundings. These are in addition to the primary characteristics which determined their classification in our Table of Consonant Sounds.

The characteristics derived from the dislocation of a primary *point* of articulation are referred to as palatalization and velarization or pharyngalization. Palatalization is typical of Russian, where /i/, a front vowel, causes preceding consonants to be distinctly palatalized. (Palatalization is phonetically represented by a diacritic, usually a raised or lowered comma.) In German we observe particularly the palatalization of the dorso-velar fricative /x/ when in contact with high-central or front vowels; compare dorso-velar /x/ in **doch** and dorso-palatal /x/ in **dich.** (The difference in the phonetic nature of the two variants of /x/ is represented frequently by a special symbol, [ç], for the palatalized variant.)

The characteristics derived from the change in the primary *manner* of articulation are referred to as labialization and voicing or unvoicing. (The latter will be discussed under the next subheading.) Labialization is the rounding of lips in articulating consonants which are in contact with labial vowels. This is typical of French, where back vowels are strongly labial and cause the labialization of a number of consonants.

The secondary features of articulation are often combined. For example, /k/ of **cool** or /d/ of **do** are velarized and labialized in anticipation of the succeeding vowel pronounced with rounded lips. Any of these phenomena will modify, but not change, the primary quality of consonants. (Dislocation, however, may be the first step toward future more audible changes in pronunciation.)

Assimilation or pronouncing in like manner. Unlike dislocation, assimilation is a tendency resulting in a change of the phonemic nature of a given consonant. This change in pronunciation does not affect the meaning of the word in which it occurs.

One type of assimilation takes place in the *manner* of articulation, occuring when a voiced and an unvoiced consonant come into contact, and the voiced or unvoiced nature of one carries over to the other in either direction. A simple example is the common pronunciation of **absorb** as /əbzɔːrb/ or as /əpsɔːrb/. In the former, the voicing of the first /b/ carries over to change s to /z/. In the latter, the first **b** is unvoiced in anticipation of /s/. The same may be observed in **presbyterian,** which is pronounced either as /prɛzbɪtirjən/ or as /prɛspɪtirjən/. Note that the assimilation moves either from the first to the second or from the second to the first of the two succeeding consonants. By and large, speakers of English either voice or unvoice both consonants in a two-consonant cluster.

A similar tendency exists in other languages. In French, **absurde** (absurd) is pronounced as /apsyrd/, **obtenir** (obtain) as /optnir/, etc. In German, all voiced stops before an unvoiced stop are assimilated by unvoicing: **er sagt** /erzakt/ (he says), **er fragt** /erfrakt/ (he asks), etc. This tendency may affect also German fricatives. Some speakers pronounce **warten** (to wait) /vaxten/, assimilating their uvular /r/ to the unvoiced /t/. Assimilation of /v/ to /s/ results in pronouncing the former as /f/: **schwer** (heavy) is pronounced /šfer/ and **schwindeln** (deceive) /šfindln/. In Russian, we find this type of assimilation in the unvoicing of /v/ in words like **povtorit'** /paftariṭ/ (to repeat), **vchera** /fčɪra/ (yesterday), and in the unvoicing of /ž/ (transliterated **zh**) in **muzhchina** /muščina/ (man). In English, we voice /s/ before /d/ in words like **housed** /hauzd/ or **closed** /klouzd/. Russians voice /s/ in words like **sd'elat'** /zḍélaṭ/ (to make) or **s bratom** /zbratam/ (with brother).

Another type of assimilation takes place in the *point* of articulation. The tendency to move the consonantal point of articulation closer to the next vocalic point was described under Dislocation. When this phenomenon takes place between two consonants, it seems more appropriate to treat it as assimilation. As an example, let us take the

70·2074

term for "getting on board of a plane," **enplane,** which is commonly pronounced /ɛmplejn/. It is easier to pronounce /m/ before /p/, since both are bilabial. Technically speaking, this is assimilating an alveolar nasal to a bilabial stop, resulting in a bilabial nasal. German shows this phenomenon in the pronunciation of **haben** (to have) as /habm/. In Spanish it occurs in expressions like **un puerto** (a port), which is usually pronounced /umpuerto/. In German, the word **nicht** (no) may be heard as /ništ/ instead of /nixt/. This represents shifting the palatal point of articulation for /x/ to the alveolar point of articulation normal for /t/.

Coalescence   This is primarily the tendency to drop one of a cluster of consonants; for example, pronouncing **good by** as /gubaj/, **twenty** as /twənɪ/, **library** as /lajbərɪ/, **softness** as /sɔfnəs/, **give them** as /gɪvəm/, or French **quelque** as /kek/.

In German we can hear **Pferd** (horse) pronounced as /fert/ and **Pfeife** (pipe) as /fajfə/. Particularly noticeable is the tendency of the sound /d/ to coalesce with /n/, as in the quick **good night** /gʊnajt/ or **wonderful** /wanrfʊl/. In German we find it when we listen to a relaxed speaker say **sind sie gewesen** /zinzi: gəvezn/ (have they been) or **Handschuhe** /hanšuhe/ (gloves). In French the standard sound /d/ between nasals has the tendency to become coalesced with the nasals: **pendant** (during) becomes /pãnã/, **vendanges** (vintage) becomes /vãnãž/, etc. In Spanish the coalescing of /d/ may be noticed occasionally in words like **abandonar** /abanonar/ (abandon). In familiar Spanish /đ/ is usually dropped between vowels or at the end of words: **hablado** (spoken) becomes /ablao/, **sentido** (feeling) becomes /sentio/, **Madrid** becomes /madri/, and **usted** (you) becomes /uste/. Through further coalescence of /s/ and /t/ some speakers pronounce it /ute/.

Coalescence may also affect vowels that are normally in contact or are brought together as a result of the silencing of an intervocalic consonant. In familiar Spanish, for example, **puede** (can), **todo** (all), **nada** (nothing) may sound like /pue/, /to/, and /na/, respectively. **Que hubo le?** (How goes it?) may become /kubole/ and **de este** may become two-syllabic /deste/. German two-syllabic verbs like **gehen** /gehən/ (to go) and **sehen** /zehən/ (to see) tend to be pronounced as monosyllabics /zeːn/ and /geːn/. Likewise, French **tu es** (you are) may sound occasionally as /te/.

Dissimilation or changing to another sound. This is the tendency to dissimilate one of two similar or identical sounds within a word. A historic example of dissimilation is **colonel** /kərnl/, in which the unstressed /l/ was dissimilated to /r/ to avoid repetition. A contemporary example is the occasional "slip of the tongue" pronunciation of **refrigerator** as /rəfrɪgɪdejtə/ or the child's /kalɪdə/ for **corridor**. This word is a cognate in Russian, where children mispronounce it as /kolidor/. French children of many generations ago might have been responsible for the change from **couroir** to the present **couloir**.

The phenomenon of dissimilation accounts for many changes in the phonological development of languages. Modern German **sagen** (to say) comes from Old German **seggen** in which the first /e/ was dissimilated to /a/, and modern Spanish **arbol** (tree) and **coronel** (colonel) come from the older forms **arbor** and **colonel.**

Interversion, metathesis, or transposition of sounds This is the tendency to inverse the normal order of sounds within a word. (Specialists in this area of linguistics use the term *interversion* when speaking about changing the position of two sounds normally in contact, and reserve the term *metathesis* to describe a transposition of separated sounds). Historic examples of interversion are **bird** from Old English **brid, dirt** from **drit,** and **curl** from **crul.** In Modern English we can hear **pretty** /prətɪ/ pronounced as /pərdɪ/ in an unstressed position, as in **pretty good.** In French, **fromage**(cheese) comes through interversion from Old French **fourmage,** and **profit** comes from **pourfit.** A present-day mispronunciation of **magasin** (shop) is /mazagɛ̃/. Spanish **peligro** (danger) developed through metathesis from **periglo.** We recognize metathesis in the vulgar Spanish /flajre/ for **fraile** (monk). Metathesis is frequent in the language of children.

Haplology, hapexy, or the skipping of a syllable. Historical linguists use this term when a syllable that was repeated in older forms has been lost in the modern form of a word. By this process, Latin **quinque decim** (fifty) became the vulgar **quindecim.** Latin **idololatria** became English **idolatry,** and **tragico-comic** became, more recently, **tragicomic.**

Synchronic linguists refer to haplology to describe the tendency in present-day familiar pronunciation to drop one of two identical or similar sound clusters which should be formally pronounced twice in sequence. Thus when we leave out /əb/ in **probably** and say /prablɪ/, the phenomenon is called haplology. In colloquial French, **substitution** sometimes sounds /sypstysjõ/, and **mois de décembre** (month of December) becomes /mwadesãbʀ/. In colloquial Spanish **pepinillos** (gherkins) may sound as /peinijos/, and **desentenderse** (pretend not to understand) as /destenderse/. Similarly, in Russian, the older form **zakoloulok** became present-day standard **zakoulok** (back alley).

Analogy   This tendency represents unconscious modifications in the use of word forms rather than articulatory economy.[1]

One aspect of analogy links it to the phenomenon of metathesis. When a linguist hears a person say /trædəjɪ/ for **tragedy,** /kælvrɪ/ for **cavalry,** or /rɛvəlɛns/ for **relevance,** he calls it metathesing through analogy. The speaker transposes sounds in saying /trædəjɪ/ for /træjədɪ/, /kælvrɪ/ for /kævlrɪ/, and rɛvəlɛns/ for /rɛləvɛns/ probably because the words **strategy, calvary,** and **revelation** are more familiar to him.

Another aspect of analogy may be observed when relaxed speakers tend to reduce the number of forms within a given word class or to create nonstandard forms according to existing patterns. When a child says **foots** for **feet** or **brang** for **brought,** he patterns the wrong forms according to **hat — hats** or **ring — rang,** respectively.

French children and cleaning women may be heard to say /ləlevje/ for **l'évier** (the sink). **Le lévier,** the nonstandard form, comes

---

[1] Analogy is also what makes language learning possible without testing every form one by one. Thus, a language student is able to pluralize new words through analogy with the ones he already knows. Analogy aids audio-comprehension of forms never heard before or heard only as fragments.

naturally to them through analogy with **le levier** (the lever) and such words as **le lavabo** (the washstand), **le lierre** (the ivy), or **le lingot** (the ingot). The same tendency to analogize was at work when Old French **l'ierre** became **le lierre** and **l'ingot** developed into present **le lingot.**[1]

All frequently heard substandard forms tend to become standard and to suppress particularly the so-called irregular forms of nouns and verbs. **Learnt** used to be the only correct past form of **learn,** but now **learned** is accepted through analogy with the past-tense ending of regular verbs.

The substandard **we was** and **you was** tend to regularize the only English verb which still has more than one form in the past tense. Similarly **he ain't** and **he don't** represent a tendency to regularize present-tense inflections of verbs, that is, to make all conform to one pattern. The form **j'avons,** used in French patois for **j'ai** (I have), conforms with **nous avons** (we have). In Spanish the past tense form **creía** may be heard as /krei:ba/ in conformity with the forms **criticaba** (criticized), **hablaba,** (spoke), etc. The Spanish collo- quial answer to ¿**Qué hora es?** (What time is it?) may be **Son la una** instead of **Es la una** (It's one o'clock), on the analogy of **son las dos, son las tres** (it's two or three o'clock).

Sandhi or alternate and shortened forms of standard pronun- ciation   The term comes from Sanskrit where **san** means *together* and **dhi** represents the verb *put.* English examples of this phenom- enon are many shortened forms not normally reproduced in spelling: /fɪču/ for **fit you,** /dɪǰu/ for **did you,** /mɪšu/ for **miss you,** /prejžu/ for **praise you,** /ɪcju/ for **it is you,** /ɔntapəmi/ for **on top of me,** etc. All these sandhi forms are considered standard pronun- ciation variants of the longer forms. They are called *sandhi varia- tions.* For example, /ɪcju/ is a variant of /ɪtɪzju/, representing a collapsing of the sounds /tɪz/ into one sound /c/ (or /ts/). This phe- nomenon of articulatory economy is akin to assimilation and coa-

---

[1] This phenomenon is also known as agglutination of the article. It is usually started by the so-called "fausse coupure," a mispronunciation in which a wrong juncture alters the word.

lescence. (Some linguists, for example, Robert P. Stockwell, do not distinguish it from assimilation. See *Sounds of English and Spanish*, p. 75.) The special feature of sandhi is that several sounds coalesce, not into one of them, but into a new sound.

A French example of sandhi is /šepa/, a colloquial variant of /žənsepa/ **je ne sais pas** (I don't know). A rather rare example from German is the pronunciation of **Tscheche** (Czech) as /čexe/ instead of /tšexe/. In Russian the greeting **zdravstvuyt'e** (Hello) may be heard as /zdrast'ɪ/ instead of /zdrastvujt'ɪ/. Spanish, to our knowledge does not show this phenomenon since its phonemic structure does not contain sound clusters likely to form sandhi variants.

Redundancy   This phenomenon makes it possible to understand a message without hearing all its parts. We are concerned here with economy in encoding as well as decoding. Our tendency toward relaxed listening habits is probably based on the fact that sound and structure signals in most sentences are duplicated to the point where many of them may easily be dispensed with. The hearer tends to pick up just enough to get the essence of the message and to miss the sounds he considers redundant. This makes listening easier, that is, the process of decoding is shortened. The shortcut, however, must not exclude certain minimal signals.

Suppose you are in a noisy room and a friend is about to introduce you to someone. He is likely to make a motion with his hand and start the introduction. You look at the person and pay little attention to what your friend is saying until he gets to the name. In fact, you may be listening only for the name, knowing that what precedes is only one of a number of normally insignificant phrases. You economize in your auditory (decoding) effort by concentrating on the essential element of the message. If you fail to get it, you ask for a repeat. This time, your friend may economize in his encoding effort and give the name alone. That is all you need, that is, the necessary minimal signals.

Similarly, a fragment of any utterance in syntactic context is frequently sufficient for native speakers. If we heard /ši:-č-ould-naj/ we would take it to mean **She is much older than I am.** It could hardly mean anything else if the topic of the speaker dealt with somebody's age.

Not being able to hear minimum grammatical signals, however, may well lead to poor comprehension or no comprehension. The grammatical signals without which an utterance becomes meaningless can differ from language to language. While **she** in **she is much older** is indispensable, the French or the Spanish equivalent pronouns, **elle, ella,** can be missed. (Spaniards, in fact, would not normally use it.) It is redundant if the hearer manages to catch the final sound of the adjective: /j/ of French **vieille** and /a/ of Spanish **vieja.** Both sounds signal that the subject modified by the adjective is **elle** and **ella,** respectively.

These are only crude illustrations of some of the rationales for economy in speech sounds and audio-comprehension. English has relatively few and occasionally not enough grammatical signals that are redundant. Compare the following French, German, Russian, and Spanish equivalents of "the beautiful foreigner" and notice that each has several signals of the gender (feminine) while English has none:

le bel étranger (m)	**la belle étrangère** (f)	
/ləbɛletrãže/	/labɛletrãžeʀ/	
der schöne Ausländer (m)	**die schöne Ausländerin** (f)	
/deršöne auslendr/	/dišöne auslendrin/	
krasíviy inostran'ets (m)	**krasivaja inostranka** (f)	
/krasivɪj inəstrañəc/	/krasivaja inəstranka/	
el hermoso extranjero (m)	**la hermosa extranjera** (f)	
/elermoso estranxero/	/laermosa estranxera/	

Because of poor auditory conditions, more than one signal of gender (or any other contrastive grammatical feature) is not necessarily redundant. The redundancy appears more strikingly in the written form, since poor reading conditions are less frequent than poor audibility.

The possibility of shortcuts in spoken sentences may also depend on the presence of a referent or the obvious relationship of the utterance to a known referent. Let us recall, for example, the personal introductions. Suppose that this time the room is not noisy, yet the person doing the introduction may not say more than *John Smith* or *Mr. Brown, the architect* (referring to a man standing before you). This is sufficient for good communication since the referent, Smith or Brown, is present. The word architect may also have a direct referent in the architecture (for which Mr. Brown is responsible) of the home in which you are or of the building you just saw or talked about. This immediate linguistic situation allows for linguistic shortcuts. It is characterized by the presence of information not conveyed by language.

Another example of information not conveyed by language is when a customer takes a seat in a barbershop or in a restaurant at dinner time. To tell the proprietor "I came for a haircut" or "I came to eat dinner" is redundant. On the other hand, if this person is at home and speaks about his grooming or eating out, he is faced with a transferred linguistic situation. Such a situation normally necessitates the use of accurate lingual communication.[1]

Spontaneity or natural grammatical shortcuts   Natural speakers of a language often neglect not only articulatory but also formal grammatical standards. Given a social situation which permits relaxed communicative behavior, we may allow ourselves to say things like **I says to him, you was wrong, he don't like it** (compare our discussion of analogy). We will be understood in spite of our particular variant of grammar. The situations in which this type of linguistic behavior is permitted are probably more frequent than the ones in which we must be on our best linguistic behavior. Native speakers everywhere often behave linguistically in a manner which is proscribed by the grammar book.[2]

For several reasons, most textbooks disregard the spontaneous grammar of the language. As a consequence, teachers do not feel free to

---

[1] Cf. John P. Hughes, *The Science of Language* (New York: Random House, 1962) pp. 156–157.
[2] In French, inversion is often omitted by youngsters in their questions: **Pourquoi il y a** . . .**?** instead of **pourquoi y a-t-il?** (why is there . . .?) or **pourquoi vous êtes.** . . .**?** instead of **pourquoi êtes-vous.** . . .**?** (why are you. . . .?).

make sufficient allowances for it. We may consider double negatives or such sound groups as **you was** to be free syntactic variants of the prescribed forms or examples of spontaneous grammar. A linguist would say that **was** and **were** are morphophonemically identical or that they are in free variation in the utterance **you . . . wrong.**[1]

Spontaneous linguistic behavior exists in any language. The teacher of a language need not consider it till after his students have a mastery of the so-called guarded behavior. Let us remember that any conspicuous indulgence in spontaneous linguistic behavior may be frowned upon. It can be compared to the attitude of those who indulge in wearing sweaters and blue jeans everywhere they go. No one can arrest them for "indecent exposure," but certain doors will be closed to them. Students of a foreign language ought not to be encouraged to attempt imitating overly spontaneous linguistic behavior, but they must be prepared to face it. They should be trained to hear, as in French, /invøpa/ or /ivøpa/ for **il ne veut pas** (he doesn't want). Similarly learners of English should be trained to hear /ajdounwana/ for **I do not want to** . . . or /jiːt/ for **did you eat?** .

Advanced students should be gradually and systematically exposed to more sophisticated articulatory and syntactical economy habits of natural speakers. Every major university has a film library which includes scores of foreign-language films. Many of them were produced for teaching purposes and are graded in difficulty of audio-comprehension. After this experience, full length foreign films may serve as a good pedagogical device. (Some are excellent for teaching civilization and kinesics.)

Recordings of spontaneous conversations are also good teaching aids, but they lack the vitalizing effect of simultaneous visual perception. To make up for the absence of visual cues, to attenuate the difficulty in audio-perception, the students may be given first a synopsis or some oral sketch of the conversation. Any nonstandard features of the speaker's speech habits should be pointed out beforehand.

[1] This concept differs from the one involving, for example, /haus/ (house) as an alternate of /hauz/, used when we add a plural ending: /hauz+ɪz/. The ending /s/ and /z/ are not in free variation. Morphophonemic alternations will be discussed in Chapter 3.

The first presentation of advanced audio-material is likely to reveal considerable deficiencies of our students. At the start, such presentations must be made under excellent accoustic conditions. At this point the aim of the audio-comprehension exercises is primarily to help the student understand the language spoken with phonetic and syntactic shortcuts. Only when he gets used to such economy phenomena in a favorable listening situation can the next step be taken — a gradual worsening of listening conditions until they are no better than those encountered in a busy street or a noisy room.[1]

There are sophisticated as well as simple means to achieve "out in the street" conditions. The whole idea is, of course, to prepare the student for maintaining a high level of audio-comprehension in the face of ambient noise, articulatory economy phenomena, and sentences devoid of redundant syntactic signals.

Review Questions

1. What is the usual name for the original language from which Germanic, Romance, and Slavic languages are believed to have evolved?

2. By whom and where were the first dialects of that language spoken?

3. From what branch of the Germanic languages did English and German grow?

4. What languages are the successors of Vulgar Latin?

5. The articulation of /d/ in **dip** is apico-alveolar, but the /d/ in **do** is almost apico-palatal. This articulatory economy phenomenon is called _____

---

[1] Even before their exposure to the native speaker's lax speech, students should get used to a noisy conversational situation. As often as possible, divide the class into groups of two or three. Let each group converse loudly, using known structural patterns for a more or less simple topic, which may be chosen beforehand. They will thus learn to cope with sentences partially drowned or distorted by ambient noise.

6. When a voiced and an unvoiced consonant come into contact and both end up being either voiced or unvoiced, the phenomenon is called _____.
   Give two examples of this phenomenon: _____
   _____.

7. When one sound in a cluster is absorbed by one of the surrounding sounds, the phenomenon is called_____
   _____. Give two examples: _____
   _____.

8. The English pronunciation of colonel /kərnl/ is an example of
   _____.

9. The tendency that caused the change from Old English **brid** to Modern English **bird** and which leads to the occasional pronunciation of **pretty** as /pərdɪ/ is called _____
   _____.

10. The occasional mispronunciation of **preparatory** as /prɛpətɔrɪ/ is an example of a tendency called _____
    _____.

11. Forms like **brang** or **he don't** are due to a linguistic phenomenon called _____.

12. The frequent shorter pronunciation of **did you** as /dɪǰu/ is an example of _____.

13. The possibility of shortcuts in spoken sentences depends largely on two factors. Name them: _____

14. When listening to an average conversation, we hear incomplete sentences, changes of grammatical constructions in the middle of the sentence, and incorrect forms of certain verbs. The tendency to speak this way is called _____
    _____.

Supplementary Reading

Dwight Bolinger, *Aspects of Language* (New York: Harcourt, Brace & World, 1968), pp. 83–99.

John P. Hughes, *The Science of Language* (New York: Random House, 1962), pp. 21–30.

Charles Barber, *The Flux of Language* (London: Allen & Unwin, 1964), pp. 60–69, 195–98, and 261–267.

Robert H. Hall, *Introductory Linguistics* (New York: Chilton Books, 1964), pp. 314–318 and 441–448.

3

LANGUAGE ANALYSIS AND DESCRIPTION

The analysis and description of a spoken language may be generally divided into four broad categories:

1. Phonology, the study of the smallest units of vocal sounds. (Some aspects have already been discussed in Chapter I.)
2. Morphology, the study of minimal units of speech that carry meaning. (Some aspects have been covered in Chapter II.)
3. Syntax, the study of the grouping of meaningful speech units into patterns we call utterances or sentences.
4. Semantics, the study of the meaning of words and sentences in a language.

This chapter will offer a more specific definition of the above concepts, clarify frequently-used professional terms, and give further insights into phonology and morphology of English and our four foreign languages.

PHONOLOGY

Phonology consists of two areas of analysis. One area is *phonetics*, which is concerned with an accurate identification and representation of speech sounds in all their varieties, called *phones*. In any language, phones may vary between geographic regions and between social strata. This aspect of phones is reflected in dialects and in the so-called cultivated and uncultivated registers of speech.

Phonetic analysis reflects also the expressive aspect of sounds. For example, lengthening a vowel as an expression of pain, "It hurts," may be phonetically transcribed [ɪt'hɜːːrts]. The aspiration of /p/ in **pin** is transcribed [pʰ].

The raised small letter ʰ and the colon are the most simple and frequently used of the many symbols and diacritics devised by phoneticians to account for minute differences between phones. (See Chapter I, "Symbolization of Speech Sounds.")

We shall discuss the phonetic aspect of speech sounds only when phonetic variants are important for the achievement of near-native pronunciation of our languages, such as the variants of /a/ in French or of /d/ and /b/ in Spanish.

The second area of analysis, *phonemics*, is much more essential for the understanding of speech sounds with reference to their function. Phonemics is primarily the study of relevant classes of phones and of the function of each class in the sound system of a language. Linguists call any such class of similar sounds a *phoneme*.

Both phonetics and phonemics are at times inseparable in the process of audio-lingual instruction. Both are included in *phonology*. In phonological analysis the spotlight is on contrasting phonemes; for example, on the semantically significant contrast between the first sounds in **think** (/θ/) and **sink** (/s/), **then** (/ð/) and **den** (/d/), etc.

MORPHOLOGY

Morphology (or *morphemics*) is the study of systematic arrangements of phonemes into meaningful units of a language. It may also be viewed as the study of the patterns by which words are built out of smaller speech units. Some linguists regard morphemics as the description of the way in which, for example, nouns change to plural or adjectives and adverbs differ. The minimal units of morphemic analysis are called *morphemes*. (The word is derived from Greek *morphe*, meaning *form*.)

Contrary to prevailing opinion, some linguists claim that morphemics is not concerned with meaning (semantics) but only with phonemic forms which speakers of a language arbitrarily fill with meaning.[1] The theory of the morpheme can probably be developed somewhat more clearly if meaning is left out.

In morphological analysis (determining the morphology of a language), the focus is on the phonemic shape and the functions of morphemes. For example, working with English, we observe that certain morphemes tend to change their phonemic shape when some of their phonemes are differently stressed. Thus **protest** /prətést/ becomes /próutəst/ when the first syllable has primary stress. The change entails a functional shift from verb to noun. More frequently, change of function is due to a more obvious change in the phonemic shape, such as when *protest* becomes *protesting* or *talk* becomes *talked*.

SYNTAX

The third field of linguistic study, syntax, concerns the meaningful arrangements and relations of words in sentences. Syntax has also been defined as the combinations or the patterns of language. In most instances, the term *syntax* is interchangeable with *structure*. The minimal unit of syntax, that is, the particular meaningful location of a given part of speech, may be called a *taxeme* or a *tagmeme* (from Greek *tagma* — arrangement). The first term was used by Leonard Bloomfield in his book *Language* (1933), but did not find wide acceptance. The term *tagmeme* is more popular and has usually the meaning of what is broadly called a slot, for example, a *subject slot*, an *adverb slot*, etc. (For details, see R. A. Hall, Jr., *Introductory Linguistics*, 192-193.) Syntactic analysis seeks the patterns in which morphemes are grouped and classifies them. This classification can differ in some respects from the traditional procedures. We shall discuss it in the next chapter.

---

[1] An unsophisticated example of such arbitrariness are the following forms: /pɔt/, /sɔk/, /gɔt/. We fill these forms with the meanings **pot, sock,** and **got,** but to the Russians they mean **perspiration, juice,** and **year** (transliterated "god"). Similarly, /gɪft/ means **poison** in German and /rej/ stands for **king** in Spanish.

SEMANTICS

The fourth field, semantics, is primarily the study of meanings, rather than meaning. This is to say that semantic analysis aims at revealing the differences between lexical meaning, which is called denotation, and all other possible interpretations of a word or utterance, called connotations. The minimal unit of lexical meaning, the definite mental image of the content of a morpheme, is called either *sememe* (from Greek *sema* — symbol) or *semanteme*.

We shall now resume our discussion of phonemics and morphemics.

PHONEMICS

Phonemics is concerned with the function of speech sounds within the sound system of a language. It is not to be confused with phonics, since it is not a method of teaching beginners to read or enunciate. In phonemics we do not ask how a word is spelled but rather how many and what sounds we hear when it is pronounced. How many functional sounds are there in the words **leap** and **bright**? The answer is three in the former and four in the latter.

Phonemes   The segmental sounds of a word (its vowels, diphthongs, and consonants), for example, /l/, /iː/, and /p/ of **leap** or /b/, /r/, /aj/, and /t/ of **bright** are called phonemes. The term phoneme has been defined in different words by different investigators. (Gleason, for example, called it a class of sounds so used in a given language that two members of the same class never contrast.) Most linguists identify it, in essence, as the minimum acoustically significant unit of speech, which is in meaningful contrast with all other such units in a given language.

Most known languages have between 25 and 60 phonemes in their sound systems. English usually totals 41: 24 consonants, 11 vowels, 6 diphthongs.[1]

---

[1] Speech phenomena such as stress and juncture can acquire phonemic status. They are considered a special category, however. To mark the distinction, linguists refer to them as intonational or suprasegmental phonemes, whereas the ones under present discussion are called, more specifically, segmental phonemes.

In other languages, the number of phonemes usually totals 36 in French, 36 in German, 37 in Russian, and 32 in Spanish. Other phonemic analysts arrive at different numbers. W. G. Moulton counts only 22 phonemes in American Spanish and 24 in Castilian Spanish.[1]

To determine whether a sound of a given language is a phoneme we must find at least one contrastive minimal pair of words. For example, the initial sounds in **pack** and **back** are in meaningful contrast, hence are two different phonemes. If the replacement of one sound in a word by another sound results in a different word, that is, if such replacement brings about a change in meaning, then the two sounds represent separate phonemes. The words /bɪg/, /pɪg/, /pɛg/, /pɛk/ indicate that /b/, /p/; /g/, /k/; /ɪ/, /ɛ/ are phonemes in English.

If a person is not a native speaker of the language he hears, he may be unable to discriminate between certain of its phonemes. Thus a French learner of English is likely to hear **sheep** when we talk about a **ship.** This is because the sounds /i/ and /ɪ/ are not two separate phonemes in French. Similarly, a German will find it difficult to differentiate between **he sinks** and **he thinks** or **he sought** and **he thought,** because the phoneme /θ/ is not part of the German phonemic system. Spanish students of English have difficulty differentiating **peace** from **peas.** The difference between /s/ and /z/ appears to them irrelevant, nonphonemic, since both sounds are one and the same phoneme in Spanish.

Equally difficult to perceive for nonnative students of English are the phonemic vowel contrasts in the phrase **What's the color** /kʌlər/ **of the collar** /kalər/ **of the caller** /kɔlər/.

The foreign languages we learn also have phonemes which some of us may find difficult to hear and imitate because we never use them in English, such as the French central vowels /y/, /ø/, /œ/ or their German counterparts called "umlauts." Consonants that English speakers find difficult are the German unvoiced fricative /x/, written **ch** as in the pronoun **ich** (I), and the Castilian Spanish unvoiced fricative /x/, written **j** or **g** as in **joven** (young) or **gente** (people). Some also have difficulty with Spanish /rr/ as in **perro** (dog) or the

[1] William G. Moulton, *A Linguistic Guide to Language Learning* (New York: The Modern Language Association of America, 1966) p. 121.

fricative variant of /g/, symbolized [g̶], in intervocalic positions as in **amigo** (friend).

Our predicament would be worse if we were to learn Hindi. In this language, unlike English and our four target languages, there is a phonemically significant difference between aspirated and unaspirated /k/. Thus /kʰiːl/ (with an aspirated /k/) means *parched grain* but /kiːl/ (with an unaspirated /k/) means *nail*. It would take much training for us to pay due attention to the difference, since [kʰ] and [k] are only one phoneme in our sound system and do not represent a meaningful phonemic contrast.

The same phenomenon occurs in the difference between prevocalic and postvocalic /l/. The initial sound of **lip** is phonetically different from the final sound in **pill**, but native speakers of English pay no attention to the distinction because it has no contrastive function. This distinction, however, is functional in some dialects of Polish in which an apico-dental /l/ and a dorso-velar /l/ are two different phonemes.

Allophones   If we listened carefully to the word **pic** pronounced by a Frenchman, we would notice that his /p/ and /k/ are not exactly the same sounds as the /p/ and /k/ we pronounce in **pick.** The German /b/ in **beißen** is not phonetically identical with the English /b/ in **bite.** The differences, however, are not phonemically significant, for they represent only a nonmeaningful phonetic contrasts. Our English /p/ pronounced in French **père** /per/ (father) and our English /b/ pronounced in German **bitte** /bitə/ (please) are slightly different sounds from those that Frenchmen and Germans would use, but not different enough to change the meaning of the words in the respective languages. If we listen for it, we will notice just about as much difference between our /p/ in **pin** and our /p/ in **present** as there is between the English /p/ in prevocalic position and French /p/ in **père.** (The first is aspirated, the second is not aspirated, that is, accompanied by a puff of air.) Similarly, you may notice a difference between /k/ in **cane** and **crane** or between /p/ in **pin** and **spin.**[1] Such audible variants in the sounds of a phoneme are called

---

[1] A visual proof of the puff of air accompanying our /k/ in **cane** and of the lack of it in the /k/ of **crane** may be given by a lighted match held directly in front of our mouth while pronouncing **crane** and subsequently **cane.**

allophones. An allophone may be defined as one of several members of a class of sounds called a phoneme. All allophones of a phoneme pass for only one functional unit in the phonemic system of a language. For this reason, unless we are made aware of them, most of us do not recognize the allophones that constitute the phonemes of our language.

Notice that some speakers of English aspirate /t/ in **hat,** /p/ in **cup,** or /k/ in **pick,** while others do not. When it comes to puffing or not puffing final /p/, /t/, /k/ in English, speakers feel free to differ from one another and from occasion to occasion as to their choice of allophones. The same may be said of speakers of other languages. Some Germans use only the dorso-uvular allophone of /r/, others know only the apico-palatal, but many can be heard pronouncing both in any position. Linguists say that such allophones of a given phoneme are in *free variation.* On the other hand, if native speakers always use a given allophone for a particular position of the phoneme and never when its position changes, the allophone has a *complementary distribution.* For example, the automatic choice a native speaker of English makes between an aspirated [pʰ] for **pin** and an unaspirated [p] for **spin** indicates that the two allophones of the phoneme /p/ are in complementary distribution in English. The /d/ in Spanish **duro** (hard) is in complementary distribution because speakers of Spanish use it only in an initial position or when it follows the sound of **n** or **l** (**mundo, molde**). Other allophones of Spanish /d/ occur in other positions and phonemic surroundings. The allophone [đ] may be heard in **padre** (father) and [đ̬] in **hablado** (spoken).

Let us conclude this part of our discussion by stating that allophones do not normally account for differentiation in meaning. Using our native allophones of a phoneme when speaking a foreign language contributes to nonnative pronunciation, of course, but it need not be a serious handicap for communication. The distinction between phonemic and phonetic (allophonic) significance enables us to better evaluate the priorities in language instruction. Phonemic errors must not be permitted at any level! Correction of phonetic details (orthophonetics), can be postponed until a more advanced stage of language learning is reached.

MORPHEMICS

In morphemics, or the study of the formation of word forms, descriptive linguists are primarily concerned with phenomena of *speech*. They are interested in speech usages by all strata of speakers, not in spelling. This becomes apparent as we consider the reasons for their use of terms unknown to grammarians of the last century.

For the study of the spoken language, traditional concepts and terminologies seemed inadequate. New concepts were formed and new terminologies coined. Because these new terms proved more practical and precise, they have also been adopted for grammatical analyses in modern languages.

Morphemes   From our training in English grammar we are aware of the elements of speech called syllables. The syllable used to be defined as the principal phonological unit consisting of a group of consonants and vowels. In traditional terms, we would say that *brighter pupils* are two two-syllable words. In descriptive linguistics, we speak of a thought unit pronounced in one breath, almost like a single word, and consisting of four *morphemes*. The exact definition of a morpheme may differ from textbook to textbook, but all linguists consider morphemes the minimum units of speech conveying a specific meaning (concept) in a language. A morpheme may consist of no more than one sound, such as /aj/, the English pronoun denoting first person singular, or of many sounds, such as in /mɪsəsɪpɪ/, the name of a river. Morphemes which coincide with a "word" are *free morphemes.*[1] Thus /brajt/ and /pjupl/ are *free morphemes*. They may also be referred to as root morphemes.[2]

The endings /ə:/ or /ər/ in **brighter** and /z/ in **pupils** are called *bound morphemes*. They acquire the status of a meaning-conveying unit of speech (a morpheme) only when bound to a free morpheme.

---

[1] According to the terminology of André Martinet, a free morpheme is a *monème* and has two facets: one is a mental image, a concept, and is called the *signifié*, and the other is an acoustic image of one or more meaningful sounds, called the *signifiant*. See *Elements of General Linguistics*, Ninth Edition (Chicago: U. of Chicago Press, 1964), p. 19.

[2] A free morpheme, in English, need not be a word root: **pro** and **con** may be used either as words or prefixes. Word roots need not be free morphemes: the roots **-ceive** in **receive, perceive,** or **cur** in **occur, concur, recur,** never appear without affixes.

In French, **nous travaillerons** /nu travajrõ/ (we'll work) consists of two free and two bound morphemes. The free morphemes are /nu/ and /travaj/. The first bound morpheme is /r/, which signals future tense, and the second is /õ/ which signals a grammatical person (in this case the first person plural).[1]

We see then that, while bound morphemes have no lexical meaning, they do have grammatical meaning. It is possible to divide them into *inflectionally-bound* and *phrasally-bound* categories. Thus some linguists refer to the plural morpheme (/z/ in **pupils,** or whatever the plural ending may be in English and in any other language) as being bound on the level of inflection. *Inflectionally-bound* morphemes are the suffixes, prefixes, and infixes of words, collectively called *affixes*. Besides the affixes, inflectionally-bound morphemes also include the so-called "replacers," vocalic changes such as those signaling plural in **man/men** or in the German **Vater/Väter** (father/fathers).

The grammatical case signals, such as the possessive morpheme (/z/ in **father's hat**), are considered bound on the level of phrase structure. *Phrasally-bound* morphemes are the forms of the definite, indefinite, and partitive articles, and certain reflexive pronouns: for example, French and Spanish **se,** German **sich,** and Russian **-tsa.** French **en** (replacing phrases introduced by nonpossessive **de**) as in **il en parle** (he speaks about it) is also phrasally bound. Morphemes like **to** in **I want to go** and **there** in **there are several** . . . are often called "fillers" and would belong in the phrasally bound category.

German **ich arbeite** /ɪx arbajtə/ (I work) represents two free and one bound morphemes. The inflectionally bound morpheme is the final /ə/. The same applies to other suffixes marking conjugational and tense endings. German, in addition, has a peculiar feature in a bound morpheme of the past participal. For example, the past participle **gearbeitet** (worked) consists of two morphemes. The free morpheme is **arbeit.** The bound morpheme consists of the prefix /gə/ and the suffix /ət/, constituting what is called a "broken" or a "dis-

---

[1] Martinet calls the /r/ a *monème*, functioning as a signal of future. Similarly, he calls /ɛ/ of **il donnait** /ildonɛ/ a *monème* signaling the imperfect-tense form of verbs in other than first and second persons plural. See *A Functional View of Language* (Oxford: The Claredon Press, 1962) p. 128.

continuous" bound morpheme. (Hebrew uses broken morphemes to form the future tense.)

Allomorphs Let us now analyze the morphemic structure of the utterance: **The hats belong to the girls in my classes** /ðəhæts bilɔŋ tə ðə gɜlz ɪn maj klæsɪz/. We can identify the three nouns and compare the pronunciation of their singular and plural forms: /hæt/ with /hæts/ /gɜl/ with /gɜlz/ and /klæs/ with /klæsɪz/. As we listen, we recognize not just one, but three sounds marking plural: /s/ in **hats,** /z/ in **girls,** and /ɪz/ in **classes.**

Our conclusion will be that these sounds are phonemically different but functionally the same. They are variants or allomorphs of the plural morph, which we may symbolize {S}. Note that we have now introduced a new kind of brackets, called braces. Linguists use these braces to denote the morphemic as against the phonemic function of the symbols. Morphemic symbols, such as {S}, usually represent several different phonemes. While the allophones of a phoneme sound almost alike, allomorphs may be entirely different from the morpheme of which they are variants. The affinity of allomorphs is not determined by common phonemic features, but by their identical morphemic function.

If, in the above utterance, we replaced **girls** by **children,** we would become aware of yet another variant of the plural morpheme in English. The plural of **child** is an example of deviation from the phonological predictability of plural morphemes. Another example is **oxen.** The plural allomorph of **ox** is obviously /-ən/. With **child — children,** a choice must be made between /-ən/ or /-rən/ as the plural allomorph. (In favor of /-rən/ is the greater similarity of the singular and plural forms: /čajld/ and /čɪld-/). With words like **feet** and **men,** one may take the vocalic change as a "replacer" allomorph of {S}.[1] **Fish, deer,** and **sheep** may be said to have a zero plural allomorph. The plural of **deer,** for example, would be represented in

---

[1] According to R. H. Robins, however, "plurals like *feet* and *men* (comparable to German *Füße* and *Männer*) can be said to have a plural formative of a zero element, and to have alternate morpheme shapes or allomorphs used before the plural morpheme represented by zero." (*General Linguistics; An Introductory Survey,* Bloomington: Indiana U. Press, 1965, p. 390.)

morphemic transcription as: {diːr} + {S}. It is to be understood within the concept of the English plural morpheme {S}, which is known to have the following allomorphs (or morpho-phonemic alternates):

/s/ as in **hats**
/z/ as in **girls**
/ɪz/ as in **nieces**
/ən/ as in **oxen**
/rən/ as in **children**
a vowel replacer as in **men**
a zero allomorph as in **deer**

The first three allomorphs are phonologically conditioned and predictable. The rest are morphologically conditioned and not predictable. (One cannot predict the form **oxen** as one can predict forms ending in /ks/: **boxes, foxes,** etc.) Certain plural allomorphs, such as /a/, /aj/ and perhaps /siːz/, could be added to the above listing, but they are found only in words of distinctly nonnative stock: **phenomena, alumni, appendices.**

In French, we find that the most frequent plural allomorph for nouns is a zero allomorph (as in English **deer** and **fish**). Occasionally we hear the allomorph /o/, as in **chevaux** /šəvo/, the plural of **cheval** /šəval/ (horse).

German nouns have a rather desultory plural morpheme. Its general symbol is {N}, but it has a number of allomorphs symbolized as follows:

/n/ as in	(**Feder** sing.)	**Federn** (feathers)
/ən/ as in	(**Frau** sing.)	**Frauen** (Women)
/ə/ as in	(**Tag** sing.)	**Tage** (days)
/ːə/ as in	(**Gast** sing.)	**Gäste** (guests)
/ːər/ as in	(**Blat** sing.)	**Blätter** (leaves)
/ər/ as in	(**Lied** sing.)	**Lieder** (songs)
/0/ (zero) as in	(**Mädchen** sing.)	**Mädchen** (girls)

Other allomorphs, such as /s/ in **Autos** (automobiles), could be added if we considered words of nonnative origin.

To simplify indicating the Russian nominal plural morpheme, we may symbolize it {ɪ}. The plural of the vast majority of Russian masculine and feminine nouns are formed with morphemes ending in the phoneme /ɪ/: /muščinɪ/ (men), /ženščinɪ/ (women), /doːčerɪ/ (daughters). A frequent allomorph is the sound /a/ in the plural ending of Russian neuter and masculine nouns: /okna/ (windows), /garada/ (cities).

Spanish nouns have a rather regular plural morpheme symbolized {S}: **casa — casas, libro — libros.** An allomorph, /-es/, occurs in nouns where the terminal sound of the singular form is a consonant: **luz — luces, mes — meses.**[1]

We can similarly recognize variants of the morpheme marking the past tense of regular verbs. Compare the present and the past-tense forms of **belong, walk, end**: /bɪlɔŋ/ with /bɪlɔŋd/, /wɔk/ with /wɔkt/, /ɛnd/ with /ɛndəd/. We hear the endings /d/, /t/, and /əd/, which are the allomorphs of the past-tense morpheme. The symbol of this past-tense morpheme is {ed}. (Note that this or any other linguistic symbol is the result of an arbitrary choice between several possible graphemes.)

In the conjugational endings of verbs (in English only the third person singular), we find again variations of the basic bound morpheme. Let us compare the third person singular of **to see, to speak,** and **to miss: sees** /siːz/, **speaks** /spiːks/, **misses** /mɪsɪz/. We hear the endings /z/, /s/, /ɪz/. They are allomorphes of the same morpheme. Note that they are phonologically conditioned and predictable, that is, the bound morpheme is always pronounced /ɪz/ if the free morpheme ends in /s/, /š/, /č/, or /ǰ/; otherwise it is /s/ after all other unvoiced consonants and /z/ after all voiced sounds except /ǰ/.

In our target languages, the alternations in the sound of bound (conjugational) morphemes are by and large predictable, that is, contingent on the last sound of the free morpheme. The following exam-

---

[1] Generative-transformational grammar (discussed in Chapter 4) offers a different interpretation of the /-es/ plural allomorph. It holds that /-es/ is not an allomorph to the plural morpheme {S} but a phonetic form caused by the underlying development of words now ending in a consonant: **luz** comes from **luce, pan** from **pane,** etc. The /e/ is thus a part of an earlier form of the noun, not a part of the plural ending.

ples are not complete, but merely illustrative. (They are by no means the final word on a complicated problem.)

In German, the bound morpheme of the third person singular is usually /t/. It becomes /ət/ when the free morpheme ends in a dental stop or in /n/ preceded by /g/, /b/, or a fricative: compare **geht, macht** (goes, does) and **rettet** (saves), **redet** (speaks), **regnet** (rains), **ebnet** (straightens), **öffnet** (opens). (Spelling **-et** as against **-t** in **öffnet** and **geht** is an orthographic reflection of the morphophonemic alternation.)

In French, the bound morpheme marking the first person plural of verbs is the sound /õ/, written **-ons: donn-ons** /donõ/ (we give), **vend-ons** /vãdõ/ (we sell). Allomorphs are the sounds /sõ/, /zõ/, and /jõ/ when the free morpheme ends in /i/. If /i/ ends a free morpheme of two or more syllables, the allomorph is /sõ/ as in **fini-ssons** /finisõ/ (we finish). If /i/ ends a monosyllabic morpheme, the allomorph is /zõ/ as in **di-sons** /dizõ/ (we say). When /i/ of the free morpheme is somewhat diphthongized, the allomorph is /jõ/ as in **apprécions** /apresjõ/ (we appreciate).

It may occur, of course, that the bound morpheme functioning as a marker of a grammatical person is not represented by any sound at all, as is characteristic of French verb forms in the singular, of English **he must,** or German **er soll.** The bound morpheme is here represented by a zero allomorph.

Similarly, the French bound morpheme that differentiates third-person singular from third-person plural in the present indicative is manifested by various allomorphs, depending on a verb's conjugation:

/z/ as in **il aime / ils aiment,**
/z/ and final consonant as in **il élargit / ils élargissent,**
/z/ and a vowel replacer as in **il a / ils ont,**
a final consonant as in **il finit / ils finissent,**
absence of nazalization as in **il vient / ils viennent.**

A few more technical terms are appropriate to our discussion of morphemics. We mentioned conjugational endings of verbs. These and declensional forms of nouns are usually called *inflections.* The term *derivations* is frequently used to describe morphophonemic changes like **high, higher, highest, highly,** or **lower, lowered, lowering,** etc.

Free morphemes put together form *compounds:* **salesman, stock market, sewing machine, cattle-raising farmer.** (Spelling the words separately makes no difference in their pronunciation as compounds.) German, in particular, tends to form long compounds: **Schlittschuhlaufen** (skating), or **Lokomotifführerausbildungsbescheinigung** (engine-driver's license). Recently, the Germanic tendency toward nominal compounds has thoroughly penetrated the jargon of American space science, which has coined perhaps the longest compound noun in English: "liquid oxygen liquid hydrogen rocket powered single state to orbit reversible boost system."[1]

French, apart from a few technical compounds such as **moissoneuse-batteuse** (harvesting machine) and words composed of a verb and a noun such as **portefeuille** (billfold), tends toward combining words by means of prepositions: **machine à taper** (typewriter), **agent de police** (policeman), **arc-en-ciel** (rainbow), etc. The same is generally true in Spanish: **cuchara de mesa** (table spoon), **estante para libros** (book case). Like French, Spanish tends to avoid nominal compounds in favor of prefixing the stem of a verb to a noun: **tocadiscos** (record player), **lavaplatos** (dishwasher), etc. Russian characteristically combines the first syllables of adjectives and nouns, for example, the adjective **vagoniy** and the noun **zal** form **vagzal** (railroad station). Similarly formed are **Komsomol** (a communist youth organization), **sovnarkom** (a kind of municipal council), and many others.

The term *agglutination* may occasionally be used as a synonym of compounding. Mostly, however, to agglutinate means (linguistically speaking) to run together, in pronunciation and writing, certain parts of speech, including articles and prepositions: Spanish ¡**Digame!** (Tell me!) or Hungarian **szeretlek** /seretlek/. The latter is an agglu-

---

[1] See "Speaking of Space" in *Time,* July 1, 1966.

tination of the Hungarian equivalents of "love — you — I," — "I love you."[1] Agglutination is characteristic of Hungarian, Finnish, and Turkish.

Our treatment of phonology and morphology, though rather sketchy, is sufficient for the purposes of foreign-language study. We shall continue in this manner as we discuss the phenomena of intonation. We shall make only broad statements of basic concepts and avoid expanding to more advanced strata of modern descriptive linguistics.

CLASSIFICATION OF WORDS

Meaningful syntactic forms (utterances) consist of lexical units or parts of speech. These units may be conveniently divided into two broad categories: open and closed. The open category consists of lexical units which may be called content words: nouns, verbs, adjectives, and adverbs. This category is open to words of new coinage or borrowings from other languages. Our target languages contain about 45 per cent nouns, 30 per cent verbs, 17 per cent adjectives, and 7 per cent adverbs. The rest, obviously a very small percentage, are words of the closed category.[2]

The closed category is made up of words which have little or no independent meaning but which play an important part in the grammatical structure of a language: determiners, prepositions, conjunctions, auxiliaries, and pronouns. They are called structure words, function words, or simply functors. The functors are relatively few, and yet there seems little need to create new ones. Such words are usually omitted from the so-called telegraphic language; for example, "Had accident send money. Hotel Continental."

Techniques used by linguists in classifying words are not based on meaning but on morphophonemic characteristics. The presentation below is merely a hint of more sophisticated linguistic approaches.

---

[1] See Hall, *Introductory Linguistics*, pp. 148–149.

[2] For more detailed statistics, consult P. Guiraud, *Les caractères statistiques du vocabulaire* (Paris: Presses Universitaires, 1953)

Broadly speaking, linguists look at the available data and observe systematic changes that most words undergo as they are used in phrases. In English, for example, a large number of words undergo only one phonemic change of the base form: /dɔg/ changes only to /dɔgz/. (In orthography: dogs, dog's, dogs'.) It does not take long to realize, however, that the bound morpheme {S} and its allomorphs can have three different meanings. The first word in the above parentheses includes the plural morpheme, whereas the second and third include the possessive morphemes. Hence, although their phonemic shapes are alike (homophonic), there are three syntactically meaningful changes of the base form. The function of the change (plural, singular possessive, plural possessive) is recognized by syntactic surroundings.

In a similar manner, English has words with three or four phonemic changes and five syntactic functions. These are our regular and irregular verbs, respectively. The traditional names, arbitrarily given to functional forms of verbs, are *infinitive* (bake, speak), *third person singular* (bakes, speaks), *past* (baked, spoke), *past participle* (baked, spoken), and *present participle* (baking, speaking). Linguists have found that a less cumbersome way to name the forms is to use the terms: *base or plain form, -s form, -ed form, -en form,* and *-ing form.* The terms reflect the linguist's concern with phonemic shapes.

There are, however, many words which show no changes in phonemic shape. These must be classified according to their normal position in a meaningful sequence of words. The process of dividing words into *nominals, adjectivals, verbals, adverbials,* and *functionals* is called positional classification.

The term *nominals* is given to words or groups of words in a position usually occupied by nouns. *Adverbials* and *adjectivals*, similarly, are terms given to words usually positioned as adverbs and adjectives. Several forms, such as English **hard** or **fast** (French **vite**, German **schnell**), can be used in the same position either as an adverb or adjective: **He goes fast** and **He seems fast.** The difference in the two functions of **fast** is determined by the grammar of the language. **He goes** is a grammatical sentence structured on the basic pattern N — V — (Adv.). **He seems** is not a sentence unless something is added to it. If **fast** is the word added, then its function is that of an adjective, because English sentence patterns do not permit adverbs to follow an intransitive verb like **seem. He seems fast** is structured according to the pattern N — V — (Adj.).

Frequently, words whose form and position are ambiguous can be identified by the help of surrounding functors. In the sentence **They called to man the boat,** the form **man** will not be taken for a nominal because of the preceding **to** and the absence of a subsequent preposition. The presence of such functors as **the** and **in** would help to identify **man** as a noun: **They called to the man in the boat.**

SUPRASEGMENTALS

The intonation phenomena of a given language are, in a general sense, its characteristic patterns of melody and rhythm. Acquiring near-native intonation is more difficult than learning pronunciation. People who are fluent in several languages may speak them all with some of the intonation phenomena of their mother tongue. This is primarily what is called a slight foreign accent. We can discern it in talented musicians as well as outstanding linguists. Language teachers cannot but recognize that many adult learners find it difficult to imitate new intonation patterns. At the same time, no one will doubt that a knowledge of the workings of these patterns will be of some help.

Linguists (at least those who follow the theories of Bloomfield) believe that all relevant phenomena of speech should be stated in phonemes and morphemes. Hence they seek phonemic contrasts not only between segmental sounds but also between the intonations which accompany different utterances. The factors that make one intonation contrast with another are then also phonemes and morphemes, but of a special kind. They are called suprasegmental since they are superposed on the segmental phonemes and morphemes. They also may be called intonational phonemes and morphemes. The suprasegmentals are rather desultory phenomena in any language and a problem for nonnative speakers as well as for descriptive linguists.

Stress   Two of these phenomena involve **stress.** If the phenomenon delimits and signals certain units of a sentence structure, it is called *sentence or syntactic stress.* If the phenomenon is peculiar to the syllabic structure of words and can occasionally signal differences between similar words, it is called *word or lexical stress.*[1]

Word stress, which we shall discuss first, is the contrast between the acoustic prominence of syllables within a word or an utterance. It can be phonetic or a phonemic.

English phrases are characterized by four degrees of stress: primary, secondary, tertiary, and weak. The symbols used to indicate the degree of stress a syllable carries are /´/ for primary, /^/ for secondary, and /ˋ/ for tertiary. No diacritic is needed for a weak stress, but some linguists use the symbol /ˇ/ to differentiate weakly stressed from unstressed syllables. In **wealthy,** the first syllable is under primary, the second under weak or no stress. In **ceremony,** the first syllable has primary stress, the second has none, the third has the tertiary stress, and the fourth may have weak stress: **céremònў.** A secondary-primary stress sequence normally indicates a modifier-modified relationship: **vêry wéalthy, ceremônial recéption, ûnknown dónor.** (Notice that secondary stress does not normally occur in sequences such as **the dónor is unknówn.**)

The four levels of stress are not absolute and may be expressed by varying amounts of voice volume. But the syllables carrying primary stress are always more prominent than the others, regardless of the relative loudness of voice.

The nature of stress in these examples may be considered phonetic. Misplacing any one stress would not affect the meanings of the words. Words like **defense** or **adult** can have a primary stress on either syllable: **défense** and **ádult** or **defénse** and **adúlt.** It does not sound quite right when a nonnative surgeon says *"it is nêcêssârŷ to opêrâte,"* but the wrong stress does not change the message. While stress in English is a suprasegmental phoneme, there are many utterances in which degrees of stress have the status of allophones.

---

[1] Dictionaries use a raised heavy stress mark to indicate strong stress and a raised light mark to indicate weaker stress. See "A Guide to Pronunciation" in Webster's *Seventh New Collegiate Dictionary.*

The allophonic (phonetic) nature of stress appears also to be present in the pronunciation of French words. While some phoneticians are of the opinion that French has no word stress, others claim that every French word in isolation has a phonetic stress on the last syllable containing a vocalic sound: **fermer** /fe-rmĕ/ (to close), **institution** /ɛ̃-sti-ty-sjɔ̃/. At best, of course, the prominence of the last syllable can be marked as a weak or tertiary stress.[1] We may conclude that stress does fall on the last syllable of an utterance or breath unit (even in the case of monosyllables): **on le cherchăit** (they were looking for him), **cherchez-lĕ!** (look for him!), **il chantait biĕn** (he sang well).

If we were to contrast English and French intonation, we would find that word stress in French is carried by the open syllables, each of which is under more or less the same stress. The contrast is heard when we listen to the usual intonation of "This is the house that Jack built," and then to the French version of that line, showing the open, evenly stressed syllabication: /wa si la me zɔ̃ kə ža ka ba ti/.

We have said earlier that word stress in English can be phonetic or phonemic. Let us now observe how it acquires phonemic status when it functions as a significant acoustic contrast signaling change in meaning and in grammatical category. We have a certain number of morphemes like **torment, combat, survey, permit** which we stress one way when we use them as nouns and another way when we use them as verbs. The change in category, from noun to verb, is effected by shifting the primary stress from the first to the second syllable: **to win this cómbat àll mùst combát.** Phonemic word stress signals the acoustic difference between words that would otherwise be homonymous.

It takes considerable effort for a nonnative speaker to manipulate the stresses. He may have to stop and think about distributing the stresses in the following: **This survey permits me to survey the issue of permits.**

Occasionally, stress also determines the difference between a preposition and a verb-postposition compound: compare the preposition in

---

[1] Cf. Lewis C. Harmer, *The French Language Today* (London: Hutchinson, 1954), p. 174.

"The wáy she cáme *tò* ..." (she came to a way) and the postposition in "The wáy she *câme tò* ..." (regained consciousness).

French has no phonemic contrasts due to stress alone. In German, stress contrasts the indefinite article **ein** with the numeral **ein**: "ein Fuß ist nicht immer **éin** Fuß lang" (a foot is not always a foot long). Occasionally it will contrast the prefix **ein** (in) and the indefinite article: **éinleben** (getting used to new habitat) and **ein Lében** (a life). Spanish also uses phonemic stress to contrast words like **ésta** (this) and **está** (is) or **término** (terminus), **termíno** (I finish), and **terminó** (he finished). An interesting example of the phonemic nature of stress is this pair: /tengolamáskara/ **tengo la máscara** contrasted with /tengolamaskára/ **tengo la mas cara** (I have the mask — I have the most expensive one). Let us add, however, that some linguists consider the acoustic prominence of stressed syllables rather insignificant in normal Spanish and even German intonation of continuous speech. In Russian, nouns like **zámok** (castle) and **zamók** (lock) or verbs like **plachú** (I pay) and **pláchu** (I weep) are contrasted solely by phonemic stress. This is of course a significant phenomenon for learners of Russian and surpasses, in learning difficulty, the shifts of primary stress in English.

As we mentioned at the outset, there is another kind of stress, called *syntactic stress*. The name implies that it functions in units of speech larger than a word, that is, in sentences. An expanded sentence may be divided into stress groups each of which is marked by syntactic stress. Syntactic stress normally coincides with the last primary word stress in a stress group or a sentence. It is usually symbolized by a small raised circle /°/ placed in front of the stressed word: **yoù were ríght and you shoùld have °tóld me that.** Notice that while the primary stress on **ríght** and **tóld** follows the usual word stress pattern in English, the additional syntactic stress on **°tóld** can be attributed to the speaker's emotional reaction to a given situation. He wishes to emphasize that his statement is a reproach. If he wishes to commend, he can use syntactic stress on **°right.** He can do both, commend and reproach, by stressing **°right** as well as **°told.** Since syntactic stress frequently expresses emphasis, it may also be called emphatic stress. Some linguists also use the term prosodic stress.

Let us now listen to the syntactic (emphatic) intonation of **I am your friend** /àjm jər frénd/ when it becomes the answer to the following questions. Notice that the speaker places the stress on the word he feels is most important to the hearer and answers best the question asked:

Who's my friend?	°I am your friend (not he!).
Are you my friend?	I °am your friend (of course I am!).
Whose friend are you?	I am °your friend (not his!).
Who are you?	I am your °friend (not enemy).

Moving the syntactic stress to another word would change each reply so as to make it inappropriate to the corresponding question. **I am your °friend** would be an odd reply to **Who's my friend?**

The same syntactic function of stress may be observed in German and Russian. In both languages, syntactic stress alone expresses the speaker's emphasis on a given word. Note, however, that in Russian the syntactic stress used in **I °am your friend** and **I am your °friend** will occur only on the noun since the equivalent **Ya vash priyat'el** shows no form of "to be." **Ya vash °priyat'el** means either **I °am your friend** or **I am your °friend.**

French often combines syntactic stress with other syntactic devices, such as word order, emphatic forms of pronouns (**moi, toi,** etc.), and the special use of **c'est ... qui** or **c'est ... que: Il est °intelligent, ce garçon-là** (That boy is °intelligent), **Qui te l'a °demandé à toi?** (Who °asked you?), **C'est °Bob qui demeure ici** (°Bob lives here), or **C'est °ici que Bob demeure** (Bob lives °here). Only a phrase such as the French for *Bob °lives here* needs no rearrangement for the purpose of an emphasis on *lives* and is normally expressed by *Bob °demeure ici*; i.e. with a syntactic stress on *demeure* (lives). This shows that French often can stress a word only by maneuvering it away from the extremes of the phrase, i.e. into the place where the highest pitch occurs. (A discussion of *pitch* follows.)

Similarly in Spanish, a preferred way of emphasizing a word in an utterance is by syntactic arrangement, such as placing the word at the end of the sentence: **Quien vive aquí?** (Who lives here?) is answered **Vive aquí °Roberto,** rather than **°Roberto vive aquí.**

Since a subject morpheme is not needed in a Spanish sentence, questions like **Que hace Roberto aquí?** (What's Bob doing here?) can be answered: **Aquí °vive** (He lives here) or **aquí °trabaja** (he works here).

Juncture   Let us now consider the following pairs of utterances and notice what makes the phonemic difference within each pair:

> a gréenhòuse / a grêen hóuse
> I am hómesìck / I am hôme síck
> They are móving vàns / They are môving váns
> They do líghthòuse kêeping / They do lîght hóusekèeping

We notice that the change in meaning from one part of the pair to the other is brought about not only by shifting the primary stress but also by a difference in the quick pauses joining the morphemes. These slight pauses represent phonemically significant boundaries between words and are called *junctures*. Junctures and the word stress often share the function of meaningful contrasting.

Occasionally, juncture alone seems to perform the function of differentiating near-identical (homophonic) word groups. A convenient symbol for juncture is $/+/$, representing a slight pause (syllable break) in the chain of speech sounds. The following contrastive pairs in several languages exemplify the phonemic status of juncture:

/ɪc+ənejm/ — /ɪc+ən+ejm/
It's a name — It's an aim

/ᵈsənz+rejzmiːt/ — /ᵈsənzrejz+miːt/ ...
the sons raise meat — the sun's rays meet

/əkould+ɪfɪšənsɪ/ — /əkoul+dɪfɪšənsɪ/ ...
a cold efficiency — a coal deficiency

/œ̃+nẽvalid/ — /œnẽ+valid/ ...
un invalide — un nain valide
(an invalid) — (an able dwarf)

/õsãde+gut/ — /õsã+degut/ ...
on sent des gouttes — on s'en dégoûte
(one feels some drops) — (one gets disgusted)

/ajn+horn/ — /ajnhorn/ ...
ein Horn (one horn) — Einhorn (unicorn)

/ɪzdañje+staroje/ — /ɪ+zdañje+staroje/ . . .
izdanie staroye — ı zdanie staroye
(the edition is old) — (and the building is old)

/es+unombre/ — /e+sunombre/
Es un hombre — es su nombre
(it's a man) — (it's his name)

Juncture is obviously characteristic of a rather formal style of speech. In colloquial speech about a familiar subject, juncture tends to be suppressed. This may lead to misunderstanding, particularly if the hearer is not a native speaker or not familiar with the topic of the conversation. The same is true about other suprasegmentals.

Terminal and Pitch Contours   Terminal contours, commonly abbreviated TC's, are the acoustic contrasts which signal either that we have finished what we were saying or that we have not yet finished and there is more to come. If the TC signals the end of a statement or the last word in a series (three, two, one, *zero!*), it is a fading terminal. Its symbol is an arrow pointing downward /↓/. If the TC is to mean "there is more to come, do not stop listening," it is a rising terminal. The symbol of the rising terminal is an arrow pointing upward /↑/.

A phenomenon closely related with the terminal is the so-called *phonemic pitch*, a complex suprasegmental and a real hurdle for descriptive linguists. Some are inclined to consider terminals and pitch as the same phenomenon and some even treat syntactic stress and pitch as two inseparable phenomena.[1]

Pitch is the audible signal that determines mainly the contrast between a declarative statement, a command, and a yes-or-no question. This becomes most apparent if these utterances are syntactically identical. Read aloud the following examples:

(1) Bob is staying in Williamsport. You go to New York.
(2) Bob is staying in Williamsport! You go to New York!
(3) Bob is staying in Williamsport? You go to New York?

[1] For specific answers to questions which may be raised by our broad statements, consult the texts suggested as supplementary reading. Read also Dwight L. Bollinger and Lewis J. Gerstman, "Disjuncture as a Cue to Constructs," *Word*, XIII (1957): 246–255.

In (1) there is a rise and a subsequent fall in the pitch accompanying the last word. In (2) a raised pitch is either carried over the whole utterance except the very end or concentrated on a single segment. In (3) a raised and sustained pitch marks the last word.

Most linguists today agree (with occasional modifications) on the system of intonational analysis developed by George L. Trager and Henry Lee Smith, distinguishing four levels of pitch. Following this system, we shall assign number 1 to the low, 2 to the mid, 3 to the high, and 4 to the highest pitch levels.

In the declarative statement (1), the command (2), and the question (3), we can then use the following notations of pitch:

    (1) $\overset{2}{2}\ \overset{2}{2}\ \overset{3}{3}\ \overset{1}{1}$ (Bob is staying in Williamsport)

    (2) $\overset{3}{3}\ \overset{3}{3}\ \overset{3}{3}\ \overset{1}{1}$ (Bob is staying in Williamsport)

    (3) $\overset{2}{2}\ \overset{2}{2}\ \overset{4}{4}\ \overset{4}{4}$ (Bob is staying in Williamsport)

If we add terminal contours, we have /↓/ after the statement and the command and /↑/ after the question. There are, however, other kinds of questions, particularly those starting with question words (*who, when, where*), which can be marked with a fading terminal /↓/:

$\overset{2}{\textbf{Where}}$ **is** $\overset{3}{\textbf{Williamsport}}$$\overset{1}{\downarrow}$ **or** $\overset{2}{\textbf{When}}$ **are you** $\overset{3}{\textbf{going}}$$\overset{1}{\downarrow}$.

These intonation patterns occur, by and large, in other languages. In Spanish the normal pitch levels in **¿Cómo se llama?** are 2 1 1 ↓. In its English equivalent, *What's your name?*, the normal levels are 2 3 1 ↓.

Notice that pitch levels and terminals refer to high and low, rising and falling intonation. They are used not only for structural signaling (statement, command, question) but also for semantic signaling, such as approval or reproof: $\overset{3}{\textbf{Glad}}$ **to** $\overset{2}{\textbf{see}}$ $\overset{3}{\textbf{you}}$ carries the message "I missed you," whereas $\overset{2}{\textbf{Glad}}$ **to** $\overset{3}{\textbf{see}}$ $\overset{1}{\textbf{you}}$ may mean "it's about time you showed up." If we feel cordial toward Miss Jones we greet her

Good morning, Miss Jones↑. If we are simply calling a greeting to
her, the contour is likely to be: 2 3 2 1 ↓.

It is obvious that pitch contours can be influenced by a number of
situational factors. In French, for example, ordering Robert to go to

Paris will be **Robert, va à Paris.** But the order given to someone

who is to make Robert go could be contoured: **Robert va à Paris.**

Contour can reinforce the comprehension of an utterance heard only
in part because of poor acoustic conditions. For example, if we catch
only the last word of **You go to work** we know that it was an order
if the contour was 2 4 1 ↓ and that it was a question if we heard
2 2 4 ↑.

Instead of the term *pitch contours*, some linguists speak of *intonation
contours*, and others of *intonation patterns*. All terms represent a
suprasegmental morpheme, a sequence of pitches spread over an
utterance.

European languages have certain intonation structures of declarative
and interrogative sentences which are unlike those in American
English. The British have usually a wider spread between the low
and high levels of pitch and let the intonation on yes-or-no questions
fall more sharply. Declarative statements in the Scandinavian languages sound to us sometimes as questions, because we associate
their intonation contour with that used in some of our interrogative
sentences.

In French, unlike English, each syllable is articulated with more or
less the same degree of stress. Therefore, while in English the typical
pitch contour is correlated with alternating weak and strong stresses
(the highest pitch occurs at the point of syntactic stress), the pitch
contour in French usually rises evenly to the end of any chain of
sounds pronounced in one breath. (This often gives the impression of
rapid articulation to those used to the English ups and downs of the

pitch contour.)[1] In longer breath units, the French contour may sharply fall with the last syllable: **Robert demeure ici depuis hier** (Bob has been living here since yesterday) or **Il n'est pas encore arrivé** (he has not arrived yet) will have the contour 1 2 3 4 1 ↓.

In German, if a sentence like

³   ¹   ²   ³   ¹

Robert, laß uns jetzt nach Hause gehen!

is compared to its almost literal English counterpart

²   ²   ³   ¹

Robert, let's go home now,

we observe two different contours. The German contour indicates, after the initial level 3 pitch, a marked downward intonation on the first word, such as we would use in English only for a terminal contour signaling "there is no more to come."

In Russian the pitch in a statement normally begins on level 2, rises to 3 in the syllable just before the one with primary stress, and drops to level 1 during the articulation of the primary stress syllable. In other words, unlike English, in Russian statements primary stress has low pitch.

In Spanish, the highest pitch level in a statement will coincide with the accented syllable of one of the words, and this gives that syllable more acoustic prominence than the other accented syllables have. If the statement is not colored by emphatic stress, the highest pitch level is at the beginning: **Vamos a casa ahora** — 3 2 1 ↓.

Using numbers as symbols of pitch levels is not the only way of pitch notation. In many texts on descriptive linguistics we find a line along the pitch levels of an utterance. The normal (mid) pitch is indicated by a line just under the letters. A line somewhat lower indicates low pitch. A line just above the letters indicates high pitch. A line about an eighth of an inch above the letters indicates very high pitch. The

---

[1] To be more precise, in Romance languages generally each succeeding breath unit (or thought unit) within a declarative sentence starts with a syllable which has a lower pitch than the last syllable of the preceding unit, but the pitch is often not quite as low as that of the first syllable of the preceding unit. See P. Delattre, "Les Dix Intonations de base du français," *French Review*, XL, no. 1 (Oct. 1966): 1–14.

following would be the representation of pitches in a statement, command, and question:

Bob is staying ╱ he╲re.

Bob is staying he╲re !
Bob is staying ╱here ?
Where is he ╱ stay ╲ing ?
¿ Cómo se╱lla╲ma ? (What's your name ?)

¿ Está enfer╱mo ?
Hasta luego.
Vous demeurez ╱ ici ?
Oú de ╲ meurez vous ?
Er wohnt hier.
Wohnt er ╱hier ?
Wo╲wohnt er ?
Ya ╱ra╲ bótayu zd'es.
Gd' e vi ╱ra╲ bótayet'e ?
Onà rabó╱tayet?

Pitch can signal which of two segmentally homologous utterances is a statement or question or what is the disposition of the speaker, but it has no effect on the meaning of individual words in the languages discussed in this book.

We should know, however, that in some languages pitch is used to change one word to another. Thus, pitch has a phonemic function similar to our word stress. This kind of pitch is called *tone* and the languages using it, for example, Norwegian (on stressed syllables), Chinese, or the language of the Navajo Indians, are called tone languages.[1]

[1] According to Nida, there is a Navajo word which sounds like /ani/. It can mean either a *face,* a *nostril,* or a *waist,* depending on the pitch level at which /ani/ is pronounced. In a low pitch (tone), the Navaho mean *face,* in a high pitch they mean *nostril.* If they pronounce the first syllable on a low pitch and the second on a high one, the meaning is *waist.* See Eugene A. Nida, *Customs and Cultures* (Harper and Brothers, 1954), Chpt. "Queer Sounds, Strange Grammars, and Unexpected Meanings." Also R. J. Hall, Jr., *Introductory Linguistics,* p. 114.

This chapter's aim was to offer a practical survey of intonational phenomena. We have thrown some light on what are the suprasegmentals in English, while touching only occasionally on those of our target languages. The suprasegmentals of each language deserve special attention through the supplementary readings suggested below.

Of particular importance are the learning problems revealed by the preceding discussion, such as the involuntary transfer of English stress into other languages. Since we have four degrees of stress, the overall rhythm of English is marked by considerable differences between strongly stressed and unstressed syllables within words. As a result, the unstressed parts of English words are often slurred, and we tend to carry this intonational habit into other languages. Let us observe our pronunciation of **captain** /kǽptən/ and compare it with the equivalent word in French /kapitěn/, German /kǎpĭtèn/, Russian /kǎpĭtàn/, and Spanish /kǎpĭtán/. In English, the natural tendency to stress one syllable in a word at the expense of the rest of the syllables is an intonational learning problem. If our tendency to pronounce words with the intonational pattern of **captain** /kǽptən/, **excellent** /ɛ́ksələnt/, **recite** /rɪsájt/ is transferred to another language, it may generate phonetic and even phonemic errors. In the French **accident** and **réciter** it may lead to the pronunciation /áksədã/ instead of /aksidãˇ/ (accident) or /rəsítə̀/ instead of /resitě/ (recite). In Spanish it may lead to /sémənə/ instead of **semana** /sèmánà/ (week).

In conclusion, let us briefly consider the role of intonational phenomena in conveying purely emotional factors of speech; for example, "a voice full of joy," "a tired tone of voice," or "an angry voice." In some instances, the suprasegmentals of syntactic stress, pitch, and terminal contours can be identified with emotional factors. Yet we must bear in mind that these phenomena are very difficult to define empirically. The lengthening of vocalic sounds as an expression of surprise, pain, etc., can be merely a phonetic variant of the normal length of the vowels. One could argue, of course, that lengthening the vocalic sound and raising the pitch level of /ɜ/ in **it hurts** to /hɜ::rts/ has phonemic significance since it changes **hurts** to **hurts very much** or **hurts more.**

Most descriptive linguists would probably agree that, while emotional factors of intonation contribute to the shape of intonation contours, they are not within the scope of present-day phonological and morphological analysis. When the tools and measurements of our analytical technique are inadequate, we may say that certain intonational phenomena become the subject of paralinguistics, a branch of linguistics dealing among other things with articulatory means of communication that are not an integral part of the functional sound system of a language.

Review Questions

1. The term descriptive linguistics covers the following four areas of linguistic analysis:

   1. _____   3. _____
   2. _____   4. _____

2. Which of the above four deal with phonemics?

3. The minimum acoustically significant sound of speech which is in meaningful contrast with all other such units is called_____.

4. What is an allophone?

5. If a certain allophone is always used in a particular position, it is said to be in _____.

6. English /p/, /t/, /k/, as in **cup, hat, deck,** is sometimes aspirated, sometimes unaspirated at the end of a word. Similarly, Spanish /s/ is sometimes voiced, sometimes unvoiced. The allophones of /p/, /t/, /k/, and /s/ in the above examples are said to be in _____.

7. If any speech unit (no matter how many or few sounds it has) conveys a lexical meaning, the unit is called a _____.

8. Minimal units of speech that convey only grammatical meaning (in connection with units of more independent nature) are called _____.

9. The morpheme of "plural" which we may symbolize {S} usually represents a variety of sounds. The variants are called _____.

10. If the plural morpheme is not represented by any sound at all, we say that it is represented by _____.

11. In what respect does agglutination differ from compounding?

12. Intonational features superposed on segmental phonemes are called _____.

13. Two of the above features are called lexical and syntactic stress. What is the function of lexical stress?

14. Place lexical-stress marks (primary — secondary — tertiary) on the following: **elevator; fundamental; generous donor; overnight guests; necessary; Where do you think you are going?**

15. Lexical stress may acquire phonemic status. Give an example from English and an example form a foreign language.

16. The kind of strong stress which divides a sentence into stress groups is called _____.

17. Which word is to be stressed in answering the question **Whose friend are you?** (Use the customary symbol to mark the word bearing the stress.) Which word will be stressed if **Where do you think we are going?** is given in response to someone's question **Are we going home?** _____ _____

18. Apart from the position of the primary word stress, the phonemic difference between a **lighthouse keeper** and a **light housekeeper** is brought about by an acoustic phenomenon called _____.

19. What are the two symbols for terminal contours and what are they usually called?

20. Which acoustic intonational signal, besides terminal contours, determines the contrast between a declarative statement, a command, and a question?

21. Using the numbers 1 — 4 according to the Trager-Smith system, mark the pitch levels of the following utterances:

> Johny, let's be a good boy now.
> Are you going to New York?
> Where are you going?

Supplementary Reading

ENGLISH

Paul Roberts, *Understanding English* (Harper & Row, 1958), Chpt. 16, "Intonation."

FRENCH

Monique Léon, *Exercises systématiques de prononciation française* (Paris: Hachette et Larousse, 1966), Volumes 1 and 2.

P. Delattre "Les Dix Intonations de base du français," *French Review* XL, 1 (Oct. 1966): 1–14.

GERMAN

William G. Moulton, *The Sounds of English and German* (U. of Chicago, 1962), Chapters 10, 11, 12.

RUSSIAN

J. E. Jurgens Buning and C. H. van Schooneveld, *The Sentence Intonation of Contemporary Standard Russian as a Linguistic Structure* (S'Gravenhage: Mouton, 1961).

SPANISH

R. P. Stockwell and J. D. Bowen, *The Sounds of English and Spanish* (U. of Chicago, 1965), Chpt. 3.

D. W. Bolinger "English Prosodic Stress and Spanish Sentence Order," *Hispania*, XXXVII, (May 1954): 152–156.

GENERAL

Harlan Lane and R. Buiten, "A Self-Instructional Device for Conditioning Accurate Prosody," in *Trends in Language Teaching* (New York: McGraw-Hill, 1967), pp. 159–172.

Robert S. Graham, "The Music of Language and the Foreign Accent," *French Review* XLII, 3 (February 1969), 445–451.

4

A
NEW LOOK
AT GRAMMAR

Every language has a grammar, whether the language has a writing system or not.[1] Grammar is not a book or a written document, but rather, as Paul Roberts puts it, "something that produces the sentences of a language."[2] As such it is the total of linguistic signals which mark the relationships and contrasts between ideas expressed by the speakers of a language. Grammar has also been called a system of linguistic traffic rules, a signaling system, obeyed subconsciously by all members of a social group. Thus we see the meaning of grammar as *a set of linguistic patterns* available to the speakers for the formation and arrangement of words into meaningful sentences.

Native speakers of a language normally use grammar without effort, provided they use it at the level of communication to which they are accustomed. This statement gives grammar a second meaning, namely, that grammar is the observance of *a linguistic etiquette*, of linguistic manners, acceptable by a given social group. The acceptability or unacceptability of certain linguistic manners is contingent on a given socio-linguistic situation. It is not difficult to picture a social situation in which "he don't know; he ain't the guy we was after" would be not only acceptable, but expected. Many speakers of English, French, German, or any other language are capable of using more than one language register and of adjusting the grammar to fit

---

[1] This approach to grammar obviously disregards the older meaning of the word *grammar*, a Greek term which literally means "that which pertains to writing."

[2] Paul Roberts, *English Sentences* (New York: Harcourt, Brace and World, 1962), p. 1.

various social situations: formal, informal, ostentatiously informal (see Chapter 2, "Spontaneity").

Grammar, however, also means the study and the teaching of *an effective analysis and description of language*. These can be pursued by the traditional method based on the original Quintilian concept of Latin rhetoric or by the structural method developed by the descriptive branch of linguistic science. In either method, we observe a systematic description of certain grammatical categories, but the means through which such categories are defined may considerably differ.

SYNTAX AND SEMANTICS

In Chapter 3 we learned that languages have a phonological, a morphological, a syntactical, and a semantic system. It was pointed out that phonology is concerned with sounds, while morphology deals with combining sounds into words. The proper manner in which the mental concepts of *bird* or *flying* are acoustically manifested is a matter of phonology. But the way in which the acoustic image (or phonemic shape) is pluralized, or understood as past or present, is largely a matter of morphology. The relationship of words in sentences is a concern of syntax, but the lexical meaning or denotation of words is a matter of semantics.

To contrast the concept of morphology with syntax and semantics, we may consider a few examples of common mistakes made by learners of a (foreign) language.

A sentence like "He brang his mother some fishes" is defective morphologically. "He some fish his mother brought" and "He fish some brought his mother" have obvious syntactic defects. If someone says "sensible" instead of "sensitive" when referring to pain, the mistake is semantic. Native speakers may find it expedient to make morpho-phonemic deviations from the standard rules (as we have seen in Chapter 2) or they may make occasional semantic mistakes, but they seldom make syntactic errors. They almost never confuse the arrangement of words (syntactic encoding) to produce ungrammatical sentences. (Using double negatives in English is not necessarily ungrammatical according to our definition of *grammar*.)

Nonnative speakers do make syntactic mistakes as frequently and stubbornly as they make semantic and morphological mistakes, because they tend to transfer to the foreign language their native syntactical system as well as their morphological habits and semantic values. Thus a French learner of English might say (possibly without any phonemic mistakes) "I am in this school since two weeks," and a German might declare "We drink always beer at dinner." They would be trespassing against the syntactical, not the phonological, morphological, or semantic system of English.

It is important to realize, however, that these systems function in practice as one general system called grammar. We know that almost every concept of the plural brings into play a relationship between the phonology and the morphology of the language. Let us recall the English plural morpheme {S} (governed by the rules of the English morphological system) and its phonological manifestation as /s/, /z/, or /ɪz/. The contingence of the morphemic on the phonemic is obvious in the spoken language. The term *morpho-phonemic* has been coined to account for this functional integration.

Similarly, there is rarely a sharp demarcation line between the semantic (lexical) and the syntactic systems. Syntax, the *meaningful* arrangement of words, normally necessitates lexical items (word forms) *acceptable for a given syntactic structure*. For example, even though **say** and **tell** may be synonymous in vocabulary, the one cannot replace the other in structures like "I'll **tell** you," "He **told** me," or "He was **told**."

If we look at a few more examples of learners' mistakes, we realize how difficult it may be to separate syntax and semantics. If a Frenchman says "at the **bottom** of the room" instead of "at the **back** of the room" he may be wrong semantically, but the mistake is also due to syntax. He is using the word **bottom** not because he fails to know its lexical meaning or because he does not know the word **back**, but because he thinks he should use it. What gives him this idea! It comes from the French equivalent sentence: "Au **fond** de la salle." The word **fond** (bottom) is the right one to use in that French sentence (not the word **derrière** or **arrière**) just as **tell** (not **say**) is the right one in "I'll **tell** you."

A combination of syntactic and semantic influences makes some foreign learners of English say "She **makes** as she **will**" (instead of "She **does** as she **likes**"), or "**Much** people don't realize how **few** they know about language" (instead of **Many** . . . **little**).

We may conclude that the *meaning* of a word is frequently contingent on where it is used. Hughes puts it this way: "When you know the linguistic situations in which you can apply this word and those in which you cannot (at least not without surprising, amusing, or confusing native speakers) you know the *meaning*."[1]

The distinction between phonology, morphology, syntax, and vocabulary has only theoretical significance and is necessarily obscure in practice. We shall bear this fact in mind during our further discussion of grammar.

SYNTACTIC STRUCTURES

The structure of a language is the system that governs the selection of words and the forms and order in which they are used. It may also be defined as the grouping of morphemes into meaningful patterns called utterances, phrases, or sentences.

A favorite example of the function of structure is a poem called "Jabberwocky," in Lewis Carroll's *Through the Looking Glass*. The poem is a parody of language. The author amuses the reader by using free and bound morphemes intermingled with meaningless syllables:

'Twas brillig and the slythy toves
   Did gyre and gimble in the wabe;
All mimsy were the borogoves,
   And the mome raths outgrabe.'

We can well appreciate the feeling of Alice (a character in the story), who declared: "Somehow it seems to fill my head with ideas — only I don't exactly know what they are!"

What we understand in these four lines of the poem is the syntactic structure. What puzzles us is the semantic value of some of the

---

[1] John P. Hughes, *The Science of Language*, p. 11.

words. We are tempted to interpret what they could mean, using as cues the several syntactic signals. A possible meaning of the nonsense forms can be guessed from some of the markers and positions characteristic of certain grammatical categories.

Thus *brillig* follows a verb and might be either an adjective or a noun: *thrilling* or *morning*. *Slythy* can hardly be a noun here, since *toves* would then be a verb with the "s" marker of the third person singular present. That would not be grammatical, since the sentence begins with *Twas* and is obviously in the past tense. Verbs can be guessed from their suffixes, such as "-le", (*spark, sparkle*) (*gimb, gimble*), and their positions in English sentences.

To show the meaning of structure in other languages, we can construct semantically absurd sentences according to accepted morpho-syntactic rules. For French, Valdman offers this sentence: *"Les galâts narpeuses mourtaient statieusement les fleunas."*[1] The sentence makes no sense, but its structure is quite clear to those who know French. They recognize the signals **les, -s, -euses, -aient, -ment,** which mark certain morpho-syntactic functions and are organized in accordance with French sentence structure.

Other examples of recognizing syntactic structure are such verb forms as *they knowed, they swimmed* or *they are baleting* /baleɪŋ/. These forms are often produced by children and prove that the child has become aware of one aspect of the English syntax. The child has recognized the bound morpheme /əd/ as the marker of past action and the bound morpheme /ɪŋ/ as one of the markers of continuous action. The fact that children apply these markers to verbs that happen to be exceptions to the structural patterns of the language is another matter. (Compare our discussion of analogy in Chapter 2.)

Similarly, children first recognize the structural function of the indefinite article **a** without paying attention to its variants. The following is an amusing example: "I had a nawful nice breakfast. I had a norange, a napple, and a negg."

---

[1] Albert Valdman, "Vers l'application de la linguistique à l'enseignement du français parlé," *Le Français dans le Monde*, No. 7, 1962.

Let us now consider the idea of categorizing the structures of languages. A view exists that languages can be divided according to their structure into *synthetic* and *analytical*. The structure of a language is considered synthetic when it tends to tie together a number of morphemes within a word or a phrase. French and Spanish tend toward synthesis particularly in the verb forms of the future and the conditional. The French for *he will speak* is **il parlera,** the Spanish is **hablará.** But Spanish leans toward synthesis also in appending personal pronouns to verbs. (This use of pronouns is called *enclitic*.): **Preparábaseles una recepción** (Literally, they were preparing for them a reception). Finnish and Hungarian are characterized by this sort of synthesizing, which is also called agglutination. German (as well as English and Russian) is analytical in verb tenses. This view of language structures has obvious weaknesses and relies too heavily on the written form of the language.

Another view of the differences in structure may describe languages as morphologically oriented (inflected) or syntax-oriented (mostly uninflected). From this point of view, Russian has much in common with Latin. Let us compare the sentences **Muzh videt sobaku** and **Vir videt canem** (The man sees the dog). Note that, unlike English, the object (**dog**) of Russian and Latin must be in some form other than nominative. In Russian and Latin, therefore, the syntactic position of the subject and object can be changed without changing their function: **Videt muzh sobaku** or **Sobaku muzh videt** is still equivalent to *The man sees the dog*. Hence Russian is an inflectional language, relying for its sentence structure on morphology (inflections), while English and French are syntax-oriented. The following are examples of the role of meaningful word order (which is one of the principles of syntax) in English and French:

> **A house dog — A doghouse**
> **A patient woman — A woman patient**
> **Un historique fort intéressant — Un fort historique intéressant**
> (A very interesting historic document — An interesting historic fort)
> **Une politique pratique — Une pratique politique**
> (A practical policy — A political practice)

In English and French we can do little rearranging of syntax without the loss of grammaticality and/or changes in meaning. In German and Spanish (almost as much as in Russian) the syntactic structure is relatively free. Particularly the direct and indirect objects enjoy much greater positional mobility than in English or French:

> **Sie sah ihn nicht.** (She did not see him.)
> **Ihn sah sie nicht.** (She did not see him.)
> **Sie könnte ihm helfen.** (She could help him.)
> **Ihm könnte sie helfen.** (She could help him.)

More elaborate changes in word order are possible in longer sentences. (See Herbert L. Kufner, *The Grammatical Structures of English and German,* The U. of Chicago Press, pp. 8–14.)

To show that direct and indirect objects may assume almost any location in Spanish, Ramsey and Spaulding offer the following equivalents of *That scene produced a bad effect on all of us*:

> A todos nos causó mal efecto aquella escena.
> Nos causó a todos mal efecto aquella escena.
> Mal efecto nos causó a todos aquella escena.
> Aquella escena nos causó a todos mal efecto.
> Aquella escena nos causó mal efecto a todos.[1]

That language structures can be categorized according to the amount of required morpho-phonemic changes in nouns and verbs is widely accepted. (We must remember, however, that there may be significant structural differences even between languages of the same category.) Since English has essentially a syntax-oriented structure and relatively few inflections, its native speakers find the morphologically oriented (inflected) structure of certain languages a true learning challenge.

GRAMMATICAL CONCEPTS

While different languages recognize the same grammatical categories, they may have divergent conceptions of them.

---

[1] Marathon M. Ramsey and R. K. Spaulding, *A Textbook of Modern Spanish* (Holt, Rinehart and Winston, 1963), p. 662.

There is little divergence in the conception of grammatical *person*. The "first" person represents the speaker, the "second" the person addressed, and the "third" the person or thing or idea we are speaking about. Each grammatical person may refer to one (singular) or more (plural) of the above. English, unlike the other languages discussed here, has (in its present day usuage) only one conception of the second person: **you.** This contrasts with French (**tu, toi, vous**), German (**du, Sie**), Russian (**ti, vi**), and Spanish (**tu, vos, usted, ustedes, vosotros**).

The concept of grammatical *number* is also relatively uniform, although *plural* is not always a matter of just one plural morpheme whose phonemic shape is contingent on the sounds of respective free morphemes. Plural may be contingent on the numerical count, with the same word having two plural forms.

Russian and Czech have one nominative plural form for two, three, and four units (and such combinations as 22, 23, 24) and another form for five and more units. In Russian the plural form for two horses is **loshad'i** and the plural form for five horses is **loshad'ey.** (The former is identical with genitive singular, the latter with genitive plural forms).

In some languages we find a singular, a plural, and a dual. In Ancient Greek, a wolf is **ho lukos,** wolves are **hoi lukoi,** and two wolves are **to lukō.** An interesting concept of plural exists in the Malayo-polynesian languages, where plural is expressed by duplicating the singular form: a ship is /kapal/ but for two or more ships the speakers of Malay repeat the word twice (/kapalkapal/). With the appropriate numeral, however, duplicating is not used.

Gender represents a rather simple concept in English. A few nouns, such as **ship** and **country,** are the exceptions to the general rule that all inanimate objects are considered neuter and referred to by the pronoun *it.* The neuter gender may also be assigned to all animals and children of both sexes.

Other languages often have strict rules on the use of gender markers. Note, however, that the terms *masculine, feminine,* and *neuter* do not refer to sex, but to grammatical gender. It is true, of course, that the word for **man** is masculine and the words for **woman** and **school** are feminine in the languages with which we are familiar. But in Czech and German the word for **girl** is neuter. Hence both languages may refer to a girl using inflections of the pronoun **it,** rather than **she.** The Czech word **děvče** and the German word **Mädchen** belong to the neuter gender solely because of their phonemic shape. Most Czech nouns ending in **-e** and German nouns ending in **–chen** are neuter.

The tendency to assign a gender to nouns according to their nominative endings is widespread among European languages. French nouns with the final sounds /-ãt/ (**étudiante**), /-tris/ (**actrice**), /-sjõ/ (**nation**), /-jer/ (**manière**), and /z/ (**phrase**) are almost always feminine.[1] The most obvious examples, with the lowest number of exceptions, are nouns in Spanish. Masculine gender is generally signaled by the final sound /o/ or /r̃/ and feminine by /a/: **campo** (field *m.*), **amor** (love *m.*), **hora** (hour *fem.*). Vocational and kinship terms are similarly distinguished: **profesor** (*m.*), **profesora** (*fem.*), **hermano** (brother), **hermana** (sister), **tío** (uncle), **tía** (aunt).

German and Russian also use suffixes as a gender signal to distinguish female from male members of a profession; for example, the word for *teacher* has a masculine and a feminine form: **Lehrer — Lehrerin** in German, **utchit'el — utchit'elnitsa** in Russian.

Some non-European languages do not distinguish gender in kinship terms. Kate, a language spoken in New Guinea, makes no distinction between the words for *brother* and *sister*. The age relationship of siblings, rather than sex, determines how they address each other. Thus /haha/ is the term a younger sibling uses when referring to any older brother or sister, and /gba/ is what they call him or her.

The concept of grammatical *case* (inflection of nouns, pronouns, and adjectives), insofar as it affects form, is limited in English to pronouns and to the genitive (possessive) form of nouns. Functionally, English recognizes nominative, genitive, dative, and accusative. Similarly, French and Spanish have no case endings, but use preposi-

---

[1] Read P. Carlo Rossi, "French Gender by Sound," *French Review*, XLI, no. 3 (Dec. 1967): 340–343.

tions combined with articles to indicate genitive, dative, and accusative cases. German has a system of prepositional articles occasionally
concomitant with case endings (**der Bruder, des Bruders, dem
Bruder, den Bruder**). Russian has six phonemic case endings and
needs no prepositional articles. In addition to the four grammatical
cases recognized in English, Russian has an *instrumental* or "with"
case, and a *locative* or "in" case. In Finnish we observe as many as
fifteen grammatical cases with such names as *translative, comitative,*
etc.

Tense refers to certain forms of the verb, not necessarily to the concepts of present, past, or future.[1] The concepts of past, present and
future action, may not parallel their grammatical representations.
We think of the present yet use a past-tense construction in: *I have
been here for some time now.* The French, however, use the present
tense for the same message. We can also express future action by
adverbs, without using a future verb tense: *He retires next year, in
two weeks, tomorrow,* etc. French, German, Russian, and Spanish
share this grammatical feature with English. These languages also
express past action ("historic" present) by means of the simple
present, especially in narration: *In 1805 Napoleon becomes Emperor
and Europe is ready to accept his rule.*

The concept of verb *aspect* in English may be regarded as a sub-
category of tense. Present-tense phrases like *He has eggs for breakfast*
and *I drive defensively* may have two aspects. One indicates what goes
on now, and the other indicates continuous, habitual action without
reference to time. The phrases *he talked for an hour* and *he has talked
for an hour* have the required signals of past action. The aspect of the
former phrase is of a definite completion, whereas the aspect of the
latter is of an indefinite completion. Similar distinctions exist in *he
will have talked for an hour* (*before you succeed him*) and *he will talk for
an hour.* Both have the signals of future action, but the aspect of *will
have talked* is of definite completion, while the aspect of *will talk* is of

---

[1] Some African languages, such as Mongbandi or Swahili, change the phonemic features of infixes rather than verbs to indicate the time of action:
Swahili for *to like* is *penda*; *they like* is *wanapenda*; *they liked* is *walipenda*;
they will like is *watapenda*; *they have liked* is *wamependa.*

indefinite completion. Equivalent auxiliaries and forms are used for the same purpose in French, German, and Spanish.

In Russian, the definite completion aspect of verbs is expressed by inflectionally bound morphemes (prefixes) rather than syntactically bound morphemes (auxiliaries). Thus **on pisal** corresponds to *he wrote* and **on napisal** corresponds to *he had written.* (For a complete account of Russian aspects, see the articles in Supplementary Reading.)

Mood (or mode) indicates a person's attitude toward the way in which he wishes to encode a message. In a matter-of-fact attitude, the mood is called *indicative.* If the person wishes to give a direct command, the mood is called *imperative.* In an unsure (dubitative), wishful (desiderative), or do-not-care attitude, the mood is called *subjunctive.* English retains only a few verb forms to express subjunctive: *I ask that he* **give** *generously, I wish he* **were** *here, I don't care if he* **be** *rich or poor.* Mostly, however, the English subjunctive mood does not involve morphological changes. In French, German, and Spanish, on the other hand, the use of the subjunctive frequently requires verb forms quite different from the indicative. For example, the French and Spanish indicative form for (*he*) *goes* is **va,** but the present subjunctive forms are **aille** and **vaya,** respectively.

Voice involves transformation from active to passive, changing the relationship between verbal action and noun without involving a change in meaning: *John sees Mary — Mary is seen by John.* (The passive in our target languages normally consists of the past participle of any transitive verb and the various forms of *to be* or its equivalents.) Within this concept also fall expressions of reflexive action, where the subject is identical with the object (*He hurt himself*), and the so-called transitive versus intransitive action: *He ran a business* (transitive) versus *He ran a mile* (intransitive) or *He mounted the gem* versus *He mounted the horse.*

The concept of *idiom* requires some clarification. Earlier in this Chapter we observed that the meaning of a word is often determined by the context in which it occurs. Idioms tend to defy this statement. The words of an idiom acquire a meaning which cannot be defined by the given combination of all the morphemes of an utterance. In a foreign language an utterance is not an idiom just because literal translation makes little sense in English. French **Vous vous plaisez ici?** "You yourself like here?" (meaning *Do you like it here?*) or Spanish **No estacionarse** "Not to park yourself" (No parking) are not idioms but normal structures with only one meaning. But French **Revenons à nos moutons** (Let's return to our sheep) is an idiom because its meaning is also "Let's get back to the subject." The idiomatic meaning of **moutons** cannot be deduced from the rest of the sentence. A foreign idiom must be translated with caution since it may, but need not, coincide with an idiom in English.

Because syntactic and semantic relations are indicated not only by the forms of words but also by their position in the sentences, our next step is to analyze sentence structures.

STRUCTURE ANALYSIS

Depending on their view of the nature of language and sentence construction, linguists speak of structural grammar, transformational grammar, and generative-transformational grammar. Any one of these approaches to grammar deals with analyzing sentences and revealing their structure. The first to a certain degree, tends to exclude content meaning from structural analysis.[1]

The basic idea of transformational and generative-transformational grammar was first expounded in Noam Chomsky's *Syntactic Structures* (1957), which created world-wide interest. Attempts have already been made to modify Chomsky's analytical theories, developed for English, so that they could be applied to other languages. These efforts represent a new striving for language universals, for a kind of "international grammar."

Our purpose is to give a brief survey of the broad concepts of "modern" grammar or, rather, grammars. In any attempt of this type, simplifications, omissions, and perhaps distortions are almost

---

[1] Many linquists cannot accept the exclusion of meaning from structural analysis. (In Bonn, Germany, a group of scholars recently developed a theory of grammar, centered on content meaning, called *Inhaltsbezogene Grammatik*.) Most French, Russian, and Spanish linguists are interested but cautious in accepting the generative-transformational approach to their respective language structures.

inevitable. We shall try and procede from the simple to the more complex, from the familiar to the new.

According to some grammarians, the statement *"Our good friends in Philadelphia have four lovely children"* is a simple subject-verb-object sentence. The task of the analyst is to identify these basic elements in single words, if possible: the subject is *friends*, the verb is *have* and the direct object is *children*. The other elements are called either modifiers or attributes. *Our*, *good* and *in Philadelphia* modify or are attributive to *friends*, and *four* and *lovely* are in the same relationship to *children*. This may be called the *modifier technique*.

An alternate, more thorough approach would be the *slot-and-filler technique*. It would identify the subject, verb, and object not as single words but as three units: the subject is then *Our good friends in Philadelphia*, the verb is *have* and the direct object is *four lovely children*. The three units would be called subject slot, verb slot, and object slot. Each of the slots may be a single word or a phrase. (The verb slot may include the verb and all the modifiers and complements that can cluster around it: "now *have* with them . . .")

The basic feature of the slot-and-filler technique is that it analyzes and builds a sentence with at least three essential slots, (subject, verb, object) and emphasizes the location (the slot) for each filler in a larger unit.

Immediate Constituents   A somewhat different approach, gaining acceptance in high schools today, is the *immediate constituent technique*. It is based on the binary principle, the assumption that most sentence structures consist of two parts: a noun phrase (NP) and a verb phrase (VP) which functions as predicate (P). Each part is labeled an immediate constituent (IC) and further divided (cut) into two immediate constituents, words or groups of words which act immediately on one another. (The ICs need not be of equal size.) Each of these, in turn, may be dividable into its own two immediate constituents.

The sample sentence used above can be divided first into two IC's: *Our good friends in Philadelphia* and *have four lovely children*. The subject becomes part of the NP (which is also called the noun cluster) and the verb and object are parts of the P (which is also called the verb cluster). The next cuts can be made in the noun phrase and in the predicate:

> Our good friends / in Philadelphia
> have / four lovely children.

At this point the three essential elements, *subject — verb — object* (*friends — have — children*) have appeared, but the cutting continues until all ICs consist of one element only.

The basic feature of the IC technique is that it divides or builds sentences in two-part units and emphasizes the immediate acting on one another (the relationship) of the constituents in a construction.

The cutting into immediate constituents explicates the difference between the structures of *The boy called up the girl* and *The boy called up the stairs*. The first cut in both instances is after *The boy* (NP). The second marks the constituent boundaries within the predicates. It separates one predicate into *called up* and *the girl* while the other is divided into *called* and *up the stairs*. The following diagram shows these cuts:

The | boy | called up | the girl.   The | boy | called | up the stairs.

Note that we can permute the elements of the predicate of the first sentence (*The boy called the girl up*), but not of the second.

The IC method of sentence diagramming is likely to be the one with which our language students have worked in their English classes. (For some years now it has successfully rivaled older methods based on the 1909 edition of Reed and Kellog, *Higher Lessons in English*.) It is, therefore, desirable that language teachers are familiar with the basic procedures of this particular approach to sentence analysis. (Especially recommended is Stageberg's *An Introductory English Grammar*, Holt, 1965, Chapter XVII.)

By and large, these procedures have not yet been sufficiently developed for application to the syntax of our target languages. Stockwell, Bowen, and Martin have come close to a successful use, in Spanish, of the procedures of the new structural approach.[1]

[1] Robert P. Stockwell, J. Donald Bowen, and John W. Martin, *The Grammatical Structures of English and Spanish* (The U. of Chicago Press, 1965).

Our aim here is to illustrate the several features of modern grammatical analysis of English sentences.

Basic Sentence Patterns   The modern grammars recently introduced in our schools present so-called *Basic Sentence Patterns* as the foundations of English syntax. While the details and approaches of these series may differ, they are based on the same linguistic principles and have a common aim: a more objective view of language and a more accurate recording of its structure by means of new techniques.

A sentence consists of a kernel pattern or a transformation of the basic and fundamental kernel pattern. The number of the Basic (or kernel) Sentence Patterns in any given textbook may vary from six to ten or more. In his *Patterns of English* (Harcourt, 1956), Paul Roberts listed only six patterns. The list was expanded to ten in his *English Sentences* (Harcourt, 1962). Marshal L. Brown and E. White identify eight basic patterns in their *Grammar for English Sentences* (1966), while Stageberg in his *Introductory English Grammar* gives nine basic sentence patterns. *Modern Grammar and Composition* (American Book, 1967), by David A. Conlin and George R. Herman, presents seven basic patterns.

How many basic patterns are really needed to represent the full communicating power of language depends on how complete and how exclusive each pattern is meant to be. It appears that only five general patterns could cover the spectrum of basic sentence structures. We shall symbolize them here, bearing in mind that they represent an extreme simplification of the concept of basic patterns. The more complete the description of grammar, the more subdividing of verb classes would be made. The symbols commonly used are as follows: D — determiner, N — noun or pronoun, V — verb (of a number of classes), LV — any so-called linking verb, Adv. — adverb, and Adj. — adjective.[1]

---

[1] Determiners are articles, possessive and demonstrative adjectives, and such words as *another, all, both, each, every, several, what, which, many, more, most.* They are used as noun substitutes (*All* goes well) and as signals followed by nouns or modifiers (*Another* man came, . . . *all* great men died, etc.). Linking verbs are forms of *to be* and such verbs as *become, feel, appear, seem, taste, smell,* and a few others. (The latter link nouns to adjectives.)

Parentheses around a symbol indicate that it need not appear in all basic sentences of a given pattern. The parentheses and the symbols within are sometimes left out to simplify the notation. The five patterns appear in this manner:

1. (D) — N — V — (Adv.)
   Ex., It hurts.
       These people talk a lot.

2. (D) — N — V — (D) — N
   Ex., I learn Russian.
       Each builder builds more and more homes.

3. (D) — N — V — (D) — N — (D) — N
   Ex., People elected him president.
       The teacher gave the boy a book about mammals and reptiles.

4. (D) — N — LV — Adj.
   Ex., It sounds exciting.
       The girl is intelligent, well adjusted, and very rich.

5. (D) — N — LV — (D) — N
   Ex., Apes are mammals.
       All Romance languages will be the subject of our study.

Notice that expanding any of the above sentences will not change the basic pattern. N — V — (Adv.) thus can represent a sentence like "Most of the old French *people* on that remote, isolated island seldom *talk* comprehensively early in the morning."

Besides the sentences whose structure is reflected in basic patterns, speakers can produce a multitude of others by combining the structures of the basic patterns. For example, pattern N — LV — N (*John will be a doctor*) combined with pattern N — LV — Adj. (*He is intelligent*) results in "John is intelligent and will be a doctor." This procedure is called structural transformation, and several of its other aspects are our next concern.

Transformations   Transformations account for the innumerable sentences we can produce by restructuring the basic patterns. For example, *He is tall* (N — LV — Adj.) transforms to *He isn't* *tall. Is he tall? How tall is he?* For each transformation (restructuring) there is a formula which reflects in symbols the procedure taking place. The particular procedure is dictated by the grammar of the language. (Grammar is what governs the producing of meaningful sentences.)

We shall study only a few illustrative samples of the formulas or rules and of the procedure by which they were developed. Thus the rule that describes *passive transformation* (symbolized *T-passive*) of the basic pattern $N - V - N$ (*The man owned the boat*) is as follows:

a. The direct object (the postverbal N, written N_2 for easier identification) becomes the subject of the transformation.
b. The word *be* with its appropriate auxiliary (Aux) is inserted.
c. The verb (V) takes the past-participial form (symbolized *en*).
d. The original subject may appear at the end with *by*.

This rule is represented by an algebralike formula that includes a number of symbols. A double line with a single arrow head $\Rightarrow$ means "transform to . . . ." *Aux* means any auxiliary (such as *have*) or any one of its forms. (The symbol *Aux* allows for a further use of morphological markers, as will be shown later.) The morphological marker *ed* signals past tense and the marker *en* signals that the form of the verb is its past-participial form. In some textbooks these markers may be printed *past* and *part*, respectively. Morphological markers are by convention placed before the essential symbols representing the stems of words. The following represents the way in which we write the passive transformation rule (T-passive):

$$N - V - N \Rightarrow N_2 - Aux - be - en - V - (by - N_1)$$

The formula symbolizes the structure of the passive present, passive past, or passive future:

N	V	N	$\Rightarrow N_2$	Aux + be	en + V	(by N_1)

The man owns the boat. $\Rightarrow$ The boat is owned (by the man).
The man owned the boat. $\Rightarrow$ The boat was owned (by the man).
The man will own the boat. $\Rightarrow$ The boat will be owned (by the man).

Note that *Aux* + *be* represents either *is, was,* or *will be.*

For French, the T-passive formula would be as follows, replacing the symbol *en* by *part* (participial form):

$$\begin{Bmatrix}\textbf{le}\\\textbf{la}\\\textbf{les}\end{Bmatrix}\text{N} \quad \text{V}\begin{Bmatrix}\textbf{le}\\\textbf{la}\\\textbf{les}\end{Bmatrix}\text{N} \Rightarrow \begin{Bmatrix}\textbf{le}\\\textbf{la}\\\textbf{les}\end{Bmatrix}\text{N}_2 \text{ Aux}+\textbf{être part}+\text{V}(\textbf{par}\begin{Bmatrix}\textbf{le}\\\textbf{la}\\\textbf{les}\end{Bmatrix}\text{N}_1)$$

For German, the T-passive formula would be as follows:

$$\begin{Bmatrix}\textbf{der}\\\textbf{das}\\\textbf{die}\end{Bmatrix}\text{N} \quad \text{V}\begin{Bmatrix}\textbf{den}\\\textbf{das}\\\textbf{die}\end{Bmatrix}\text{N} \Rightarrow$$

$$\begin{Bmatrix}\textbf{der}\\\textbf{das}\\\textbf{die}\end{Bmatrix}\text{N}_2 \text{ Aux}+\textbf{werden} (\textbf{von}\begin{Bmatrix}\textbf{dem}\\\textbf{der}\\\textbf{den}\end{Bmatrix}\text{N}_1) \text{ part}+\text{V}$$

A T-passive procedure for Spanish is suggested in an article by Bela Banathy and others, of which the following is a modified example including a structural string.[1]

$$\text{N V D N} \Rightarrow \text{D N}_2 \text{ Aux}+\textbf{ser part}+\text{V (\textbf{por} N}_1)$$

Todos temían la situación $\Rightarrow$ D N$_2$ past$+$**ser** part$+$V **por** N$_1$

> **la** — **situación** — **fué** — part$+$**temer** — **por** — **todos**
> **La situación fué temida por todos.**

Todos temían la situación (All feared the situation)

N$_1$ — V — D — N$_2$ $\Rightarrow$

D-N$_2$ — Aux — **ser** — part — V — (**por** — N$_1$)

D-N$_2$ — past$+$**ser** — part$+$V — **por** — N$_1$

la — **situación** — **fué** — part$+$**temer** — **por** — **todos**
La situación fué temida por todos.
(The situation was feared by all.)

This example (and to a certain degree also the example for French and German) does not, of course, represent an all-inclusive formula.

---

[1] See Albert Valdman, ed., *Trends in Language Teaching* (New York: McGraw-Hill, 1966), pp. 41–43.

An application of the rewritten formula is demonstrated in the following example of *Yes/No Question Transformation* (symbolized *T — yes/no*).

The formula reflects the procedure of transforming a sentence pattern N — V — N, in which V is expanded by an auxiliary (Aux), to a yes/no question, such as the transformation of *He could have repaired them* to *Could he have repaired them?* The procedure occurs in three steps. First the basic formula showing the inclusion of *Aux* and the structure of the transforms:

$$N — Aux — V — N \Rightarrow Aux — N — (remaining\ Aux) — V — N$$

Second the representation (rewriting) of the possible components of *Aux* (first the left side, then the right side of the above formula):

$$N — Aux \rule{4cm}{0.4pt} V — N \Rightarrow$$

LEFT
$$N — \begin{Bmatrix} -\emptyset \\ -s \\ -ed \end{Bmatrix} — (Modal) — (have — en) — (be+ing)$$
$$— V — N \Rightarrow$$

The symbol $\emptyset$ represents an unmodified form of the subsequent modal or verb, and the symbols *-s* and *-ed* represent the forms of the third person singular and of the past tense, respectively.

$$Aux \rule{5cm}{0.4pt}$$
$$N — (remaining\ Aux) — V — N$$

RIGHT
$$\begin{Bmatrix} -\emptyset \\ -s \\ -ed \end{Bmatrix} — (Modal) — (have — en) — (be+ing)$$
$$— N — (remaining\ Aux) — V — N$$

The third step is to rewrite first the left and then the right sides of this transformation formula in the form of structural strings, which show the specific selection made from the possible choices within the braces and the parentheses:

LEFT
he	ed+Modal — (have — en) — repair — them
he	ed+can — have — en + repair — them
He	*could* *have* *repaired* *them.*

RIGHT
-ed — (Modal) — he — (have — en) — repair	— them
-ed + can — he — have — en + repair	— them
Could *he* *have* *repaired*	*them?*

The choice of -Ø and of (be+ing), instead of -ed and (have — en), would be obvious in a sentence like *Will we be repairing them?* The structural string then would be developed from the formula as follows:

Aux   N — (remaining Aux) — V — N

$\begin{Bmatrix} \text{Ø} \\ \text{-s} \\ \text{-ed} \end{Bmatrix}$ — (Modal) — (have — en) — (be+ing)

                                            — N — (remaining Aux) — V — N

0+(Modal) — _____ — we — (be — ing) — repair — them
0+will   —   we — be — ing + repair — them
Will   *we   be   repairing   them?*

When the Yes/No Question Transformation rule is applied to English sentences with no Modal, we must introduce *do* as a support word. Note the transformation of *He repairs cars* to *Does he repair cars?* In such cases the formula is written this way:

$$\text{N — V — N} \Rightarrow \begin{Bmatrix} \text{Ø} \\ \text{-s} \\ \text{-ed} \end{Bmatrix} \text{— do — N — V — N — (remainder of sentence)}$$

The right side can be rewritten into a structural string as follows:

s+do — he — repair — cars
Does   he   repair   cars?

We have now at least a general idea about the procedures of transforming basic sentences to the passive and to yes/no question structures. In a similar way (though occasionally more complicated), transformational grammar presents rules of transformation for *WH* (where, when, what, who) *questions,* and negative, imperative, and negative imperative structures. Any syntactic rearrangement and any generating of complex sentences from the basic patterns may be represented by a rule expressed in a formula.

The theory of the generative-transformational grammar is complex and not easy to explain in a sketchy manner. Its complexity, however, is justified by the explicit answers it claims to offer to certain questions of syntax.

Explicitness, which is the principal aim of the new approach, means describing the process of sentence formation in precise detail. When this aim is fully achieved, a machine, using the generative and trans-formational formulas of rules could eventually generate an infinite number of grammatical sentences. In other words, the syntax of a language could be duplicated with accuracy by following explicit descriptive rules, without the application of native linguistic *intuitions*.

At present, not all the generative-transformational rules are work-able in every given linguistic situation, but scholars are hard at work to perfect the technique. According to Chomsky, their task is to present an explicit analysis of what is involved in a native speaker's "application of intelligence" to the data of the grammar. Much of this research, particularly experimental modifications of the tech-nique pertinent for other languages, can now be found in yet unpublished doctoral dissertations.[1]

An example of the generative-transformational technique of sentence analysis is given below.[2] The sentences to be analyzed are:

> (A) I persuaded John to leave.
> (B) I expected John to leave.

On the surface, the structure of (A) and (B) appears syntactically identical. We sense, however, that there is an underlying structural difference, apart from the obvious lexical difference, between **per-suaded** and **expected.**

The theory considers sentence (A) a transformational derivation of two basic sentences:

> (1) *I persuaded John* and
> (2) *John leaves* (the leaving of John).

Similarly, sentence (B) is considered a transformation of

> (3) *I expected* and
> (4) *John leaves.*

---

[1] A readable and informative dissertation, available on microfilm, is that of David L. Wolfe, "A Generative-Transformational Analysis of Spanish Verb Forms" (Ann Arbor: University Microfilms, 1966). I am indebted to Dr. Wolfe for several items of information.

[2] The example is based on the technique of Noam Chomsky, *Aspects of the Theory of Syntax* (Cambridge, Mass.: M.I.T. Press, 1965), p. 22.

In sentence (A), **John** is the object of **persuaded** and of **leave.** In (3), the verb **expected** has no direct object and in (4), which may be considered an added subordinate clause, **(that) John leaves,** John is the subject. Hence the subsurface structures of (A) and (B) are not identical.

Another illustration of the difference is the following:

(A) can be changed to *I persuaded John that he (should) leave.*

(B) cannot be changed to *I expected John that he (should) leave.*

The rule of transformation will render (B) as

$$I\ expected\ that\ John\ (would)\ leave.$$

Note that the Immediate Constituant technique would not reveal the difference in the structures of *I persuaded John to leave* and *I expected John to leave.*

The generative transformational technique can thus make explicit a number of grammatical phenomena hitherto not explained but only intuitively felt by native speakers.

Let us summarize by saying that *modern grammar* is generally viewed as a partially organized body of rules which describe a system of grammatical sentences, assigning to each sentence its precise structural description. The pragmatic reason for new procedures in analyzing sentences is to find the best possible way for a beginning language learner to see the structure of the target language.

The structural approach, which is typical on the American linguistic scene, is characterized by regarding language as structure. Leonard Bloomfield, who is often called the father of American linguistic studies, considers language as a structure made up of units, of which the smallest and most basic one is a phoneme.

Chomsky, who is the leader of generative-transformational grammarians, considers language as behavior governed by structural rules. His theory attempts to explain how a limited number of structure patterns (kernel sentences) generates an unlimited number of sentences through the rule-governed use of transformations.

The efforts of modern grammarians have been also directed toward an understanding of the subsurface grammar (structure) of a language. The subsurface grammar is something that produces the structural difference between sentences that appear syntactically identical on the surface level of analysis. Example:

> He is eager to please.
> He is easy to please.

The subsurface structure of the two sentences conveys the underlying action by the subject described as *eager* and the non-action by the subject described as *easy*.

The deep structural phenomena of language not noticed in the surface structure are also explored by an approach or method called *tagmemics*. Tagmemic analysis is a sophisticated slot-and-filler technique attempting to define the subsurface classifications of concepts in a language system. (A *tagmeme*, as a grammatical unit, is the correlation of a grammatical function or slot with a class of mutually substitutable items occurring in that slot.) The tagmemic method appears to be suited for the analysis of so-called exotic languages, whose structure is completely foreign to native speakers of major Western languages.[1]

To discuss the differences between the school of structural and the school of transformational linguistics would require considerable space. By and large, the structuralists claim that language is a social habit acquired by imitation. To acquire this habit later in life, one must study the phonemes of a language and the system whereby they are arranged into messages. This system, generally called grammar, is far more flexible than traditional grammarians would admit. Structuralists advocate that whichever way native speakers choose to construct their messages is necessarily the right way.

Transformationalists claim that a concept of language based on imitation alone is inadequate. Native speakers, to varying degrees,

---

[1] See Benjamin Elson and V. Pickett, *An Introduction to Morphology and Syntax* (Santa Barbara: Summer Institute of Linguistics, 1967). This work offers a good introduction to tagmemic analysis, even though it treats mainly American-Indian languages.

are able to draw upon an innate linguistic intuition which can guide them to an infinite number of constructions they never heard before. To acquire the linguistic competence of native speakers, an adult learner of the language, in addition to discerning the given sounds of a sentence, must master the rules that enable him to give the sentence a specific meaning. Hence any spoken utterance is analyzed on its surface (what one hears) as well as on its subsurface level (the level of meaning).

According to an article in *Time* magazine, a structuralist argues that his is a scientific approach, whereas the approach of the transformationalist is like "the speculations of a neo-medieval philosopher."[1]

The ideas of the transformationalists regarding subsurface analysis have earned them considerable recognition among researchers in related fields, notably psychology, but they have proved thus far less adaptable to language teaching. It is mainly the surface level of transformational analysis that led to the use of substitution and transformation drills. The applied linguistics method or what is often termed the "new key" method appears to be based rather on the findings of the structural approach to the analysis of languages. For example, the use of minimal contrastive pairs (see next chapter) reflects the structuralists' concept of the role of the phoneme.

The conclusion to be drawn by all those interested in language teaching techniques is simply that the study of grammar cannot be underestimated and is by no means oldfashioned. It should be remembered at all levels of our teaching that "grammar" is what produces meaningful sentences in a language. Knowing the phonemic system is important, of course, but of little value is a flawless pronunciation if the student does not know on what to use it. Grammar is needed to perform adequately in listening and speaking.

[1] Charles F. Hocket, quoted in *Time*, February 16, 1968, p. 69. A brief, authoritative survey of the history of descriptive linguistics on the European and American scenes is presented in Gleason's *Linguistics and English Grammar* pp. 76–86.

Review Questions

1. The mistakes made by a learner of a foreign language can be categorized as:

   a. phonological
   b. morphological
   c. syntactic
   d. semantic

   Give an English example of each of the above categories of mistakes:

   a. _____
   b. _____
   c. _____
   d. _____

2. Even uneducated native speakers make hardly any mistakes in which of the above categories?

3. Grammar can be defined as a study of an effective analysis and description of language. What other definitions of grammar do linguists offer?

4. Structure may be defined as _____.

5. What are the phonological manifestations of the plural morpheme in English?

6. We can identify (recognize) nouns and verbs in a sentence because of certain structural signals. Name some: _____
   _____

7. It has been said that some languages are morphologically oriented and others are syntax-oriented. Name one language of the latter group and give two examples of a syntax-oriented grammar: _____
   _____

8. What is an idiom?

9. What is the basic feature of the slot-and-filler technique?

10. What is the basic feature of the IC technique?

11. Employing the IC technique, make the first two cuts in:
    He looked up the strange chimney.
    He looked up the strange word.

12. Speaking of the "new grammar," the form *would* consists of the tense marker _____ plus the modal *will*.

13. *Has* consists of _____ plus *have*.

14. The string *he — ed — shall — leave* is rewritten _____.

15. Rearrange the string *he — ed — shall — leave* into a string representing a yes/no question.

16. What is the transformation rule applied to the yes/no question structure without a modal?
    T — yes/no: N — V — N ⇒

Supplementary Reading

BOOKS

Frederick Bodmer, *The Loom of Language*, (New York: Norton, 1944) Chapter 4.

Henry A. Gleason, Jr., *Linguistics and English Grammar* (New York: Holt, 1965), Chapters 7, 10–12.

Norman C. Stageberg, *An Introductory English Grammar* (New York: Holt, 1967) Chapters 15–17.

Dwight Bolinger, *Aspects of Language* (New York: Harcourt, Brace, & World), pp. 184–212.

ARTICLES

Sol Saporta, "Applied Linguistics and Generative Grammar," in *Trends in Language Teaching* (New York: McGraw-Hill, 1967), 81–91.

Dona W. Brown, *et al.*, "Grammar in a New Key," reprinted in *Essays on Language and Usage*, 2nd ed. (New York: Oxford U. Press, 1963), 210–216.

Frances de Graaff, "The Verbal Aspect in Russian," *Modern Language Journal*, XXVI (May 1952): 220–222.

Harry H. Josselson, "On Teaching the Aspect of The Russian Verb," *Language Learning*, I (Oct. 1948): 3–8.

Roger Brown & U. Bellugi, "Three Processes in the Child's Acquisition of Syntax" and Susan Ervin, "Imitation and Structural Change in Children's Language," in *New Directions in the Study of Language*, Eric H. Lenneberg, ed. (Cambridge, Mass.: The M.I.T. Press, 1966), pp. 131–188.

Simon Belasco, "Les structures grammaticales orales," in *Le Français dans le Monde*, 41 (juin, 1966), 37–46.

5

PRACTICAL HINTS: PHONEMICS

PHONEMIC DIFFICULTIES

During the process of second-language learning, the student encounters a number of difficulties which are caused by various predictable factors. The order in which these difficulties become apparent and their relative intensity depend to a large extent on the method by which he is learning a language.

Assuming that the method is audio-lingual, certain difficulties in functional sounds will be encountered early.[1] All phonemes of the second language that are new to the learner's ear, in the sense that he never hears them in English, are likely to present stubborn auditory and thus also articulatory problems.

It is pedagogically advisable that the student be helped to develop awareness of these new sounds before his attention is absorbed by problems of morphology, meaning, and syntax. In other words, a short phonemic training phase should precede the learning of dialogues. Even the very simple dialogue inevitably integrates the learning of word forms, word meaning, and word order. This integration has its desirable aspects, provided the learner is not frustrated by sounds he cannot discern and imitate.

There is only one group of learners, the very young, the geniuses in our society when it comes to language learning, who have no auditory discernment and mimicry problems. They have such facility in hear-

[1] The reading and writing method presents primarily problems of orthography (particularly in languages using non-Latin alphabets), of sentence structure, and of false cognates.

ing and articulating new sounds that no systematic exercises are necessary for them. Pupils who are eight or little older already show genuine auditory and articulatory difficulties when starting a new language. There are, of course, individual differences, and we may find adults who have no difficulty discerning and imitating new sounds.

At the start of the phonemic phase, let us introduce the idea that the new language is not a string of printed words but a string of sounds. Many of the sounds are almost like those of our native language, but there are some which are quite different. We pick out these sounds in a certain order and listen to them with extra attention. Then we give each a phonemic symbol designed to evoke the sound more effectively than conventional orthography. Sounds entirely absent from the learner's own language are relatively few.

Identification of the new sounds is, of course, only the first step. To be meaningful and more learnable, sounds must be listened to and articulated in words. To make their particular acoustic quality clearly noticeable, we use the device of contrasting one word against another.

Minimal Contrastive Pairs   A good foreign-language textbook or a well-designed course should contain material for oral practice designed to teach the student to hear and articulate those phonemes which do not exist in his native sound system. Obviously, the same or appropriately modified material should be available on tapes for the language laboratory.

This material normally consists of selected words arranged in series according to certain acoustic contrasts. There are two basic kinds of such series. One kind uses the student's native words contrasted with the words of the foreign language. These word contrasts form bilingual pairs. The other kind presents sound contrasts in words of the foreign language alone. These form monolingual pairs.

In either kind of series, each pair consists of words that differ by a minimal number of phonemes, preferably by only one. Hence the usual name for this material is minimal contrastive pairs, or simply, minimal pairs.

Minimal pairs are typical of language teaching influenced by linguistics. They cannot solve all problems of phonology, but they are more effective than less professional devices that we may hear about. For example, this is what was suggested to a foreign student who could not hear the difference between such words as *view* and *few*: "Say 'a beautiful view,' 'the view from my window' until you can practically see the word as you hear it."[1] Then he was to do the same thing with *few*.

We know from experience that repeating a word in context does not reveal the phonemic value of a specific sound, particularly if the sound is not a phoneme in the student's native language. The sounds /v/ and /f/ were obviously not two separate phonemes in the language of the above foreign student.

An informed language teacher would ask the student with such a problem to procede as follows:

(1) Look for your native words which start with a sound like the one you hear in *view* or *few*. Select those that are one-syllabic.
(2) Contrast these words with English words like *few, fine* and *view, vine*, while you hear them pronounced by a native speaker of English.
(3) Practice hearing and repeating such minimal pairs as these:

| few / view | feel / veal | fat / vat |
| fine / vine | fan / van | fail / veil |

In this chapter, as the minimal contrastive pairs are introduced, we generally take the position that English has acceptable counterparts for the majority of the phonemes of a given language and that most allophonic differences causing a foreign accent are not a pressing problem. This position is not shared by all members of the profession, but it is supported by many experienced language teachers who are inclined to be tolerant of the problems facing beginning students. The following is a concise statement of this position:

"For ordinary communication purposes, the main goal of foreign language study in the twentieth century, a foreign accent need

---

[1] Leslie J. Nason, "There's a Recognizable Difference in Sounds," Nason on Education Column, AP News Features, March 13, 1968.

not be eliminated, unless the learner is young and can eliminate it without having to pay an excessive price in time and effort at the expense of other aspects of the language."[1]

Let us assume that the learner has neither the advantage of a child nor the time necessary to reach the level of native pronunciation, while he strives for an ability to communicate in the foreign language. Our aim is to present brief explanations of the articulation of certain sounds and to introduce standard examples of minimal contrastive pairs. The pairs are designed to reveal the phonemic qualities of sounds that present learning problems because they do not occur in English. Each set of pairs is intended to fix in the learner's mind a specific phoneme absent from the English phonemic system. So that this may be accomplished, the set should contain an optimal number of pairs. The more difficult the foreign sound, the more pairs may be needed. Examples given here average about four pairs to a set. In most cases, this number should be doubled in actual practice.

Bilingual Pairs   A bilingual set of minimal pairs focuses on a single phonological problem. A set designed to make the learner discern, for example, the French or the German sound /y/ will include English-French pairs, such as **loot** / **lutte** (fight), or English-German pairs, such as **tour** / **Tür** (door). Here is what the learner must do to get the most out of the exercise:

(1) Articulate the familiar sound in a short English word.
(2) Listen carefully for the difference between the English sound and the foreign sound in a minimal pair.
(3) Articulate the foreign sound in a short word from the target language. At this point, the learner should look at the face of the native model, if possible.
(4) Be aware of the differences in the point and manner of articulation between the English sound and the foreign sound. This can be facilitated by the instructor's explanation and by sketches, such as those shown on page 117. (The older the learner, the more he is likely to appreciate a linguistic explanation.)

[1] Robert Lado, *Language Testing* (New York: McGraw-Hill, 1964), p. 40.

Bearing the above instructions in mind, we can now study bilingual contrastive pairs.

English / French   The French /ʀ/ is a dorso-uvular fricative and may be produced in the following manner: The student repeats the sounds /ag/, making them as short as possible. Then, still keeping the tip of the tongue against the lower teeth, he gradually ceases to make the occlusion of /g/ until he produces a fricative. He is then saying /aʀ/ as in **devoir** or in **parle.** Next we ask him to keep his tongue in the same position (apex against the lower teeth) and repeat the sounds /ʀa/ as if he were gargling, using as little breath as possible. When he is able to produce the initial sound /ʀ/, as in **rabat** we can make him appreciate the difference between American /r/ and French /ʀ/ in pairs like these:

fair	/feər/	/fɛːʀ/	faire
pair	/peər/	/pɛːʀ/	pair
rare	/reər/	/ʀaːʀ/	rare
route	/rut/	/ʀut/	route

French /y/, /œ/, and /ø/ pose the following problems: In English, the rounded vowels are the back vowels /ɔ/, /o/, and /u/. In French, some central vowels are also articulated with distinctly rounded lips. English, too, has a central vowel, the so-called reduced vowel /ɜ/ as in **bird,** which is occasionally articulated with a slight rounding of the lips and can sound, to an untrained listener, as any one of the three French vowels we are discussing. It is thus likely that a student of French may mistakenly hear and articulate /ɜ/, instead of /y/ /œ/, or /ø/. (Think of the frequent mispronunciation of **soeur** as /sɜr/ or **dur** as /dɜr/.)

To produce /y/, the student may start with his tongue in the position for /ɪ/ as in **lit,** but change the position of his lips from spread to considerably rounded. Or he may start with the lips in the rounded position for /u/ as in **loot,** but move his tongue forward and slightly downward. These positions of tongue and lips should produce the sound /y/ in French **lutte.** Then he can contrast the sounds /u/ and /y/ in pairs such as these:

loot	/lut/	/lyt/	luth	
poor	/pur/	/pyʀ/	pure	HIGH — CENTRAL,
shoot	/šut/	/šyt/	chute	ROUNDED /y/
flute	/flut/	/flyt/	flute	(Sketch 1)
plume	/plum/	/plym/	plume	

He can also practice triplets of English-French-English words, such as these:

loot	lutte /lyt/	lit
boot	but /byt/	bit

Similarly with the sound /œ/, in which case the starting positions may be that for either /ɛ/ as in **bear** or /ɔ/ as in **bore.** Practice contrasting /ɔ/ with /œ/ in pairs such as these:

pore	/pɔr/	/pœʀ/	peur	
core	/kɔr/	/kœʀ/	cœur	MID-CENTRAL,
sore	/sɔr/	/sœʀ/	sœur	SEMIROUNDED /œ/
bore	/bɔr/	/bœʀ/	beurre	(Sketch 2)
lore	/lɔr/	/lœʀ/	leur	

Some students may benefit from contrasting /ʌ/, as in **club,** with /œ/ in such French words as **club** /klœb/ and other borrowings. Other students may prefer to work with English-French-English triplets:

pore	peur /pœʀ/	pair
core	cœur /kœʀ/	care

To produce /ø/, the starting position is that for English /u/, as in **shoe** or **crew.** The point of articulation for /ø/ is then moved slightly lower and forward. To become aware of the contrast between /u/ and /ø/, the student may use pairs like **crew** /kru/ — **creux** /kʀø/. In rapid, informal speech, some speakers of French tend not to distinguish clearly the sounds /œ/ and /ø/. While the distinction is certainly not on its way out of the French phonemic system, this lack of native clarity allows us to simplify the initial phonemic training of our students. Instead of insisting on the distinction between /œ/ as in **neuf** and /ø/ as in **neutre,** we can choose just one of the two sounds for initial practice. The sound /œ/ is easier to mimic, since it does not require the very tense articulation characteristic of /ø/.

Facial Sketches[1]

1

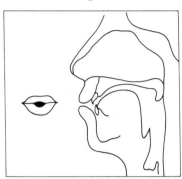

High-central, rounded /y/
French: lune, bus, début
German: fünf, müssen, kühn

2

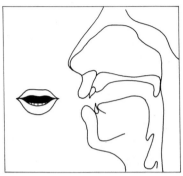

Mid-central, semirounded /œ/
French: œuvre, bœuf, fleuve
German: öffnen, Hölle, Köln

3

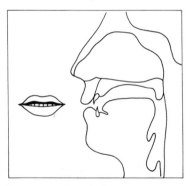

Dorso-uvular /ʀ/
French: radio, revoir, Robert
German: Radio, Rose, Rohre

4

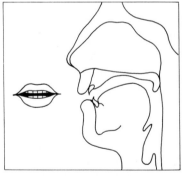

Dorso-velar, unvoiced /x/ or
   voiced /g/
German: China, suchen, doch
Russian: ход, дух, чех
Spanish: jefe, pagar

[1] These sketches are based on those of Prof. B. Hála, reproduced by permission of the Statní pedagogické nakladatelství, Prague, Czechoslovakia.

(See our examples of monolingual pairs and the treatment of /ø/ in the next chapter.)

In French /õ/, /ã/, /ɛ̃/, /œ̃/, the peculiar quality of these vowels results from nasalization that is simultaneous with the articulation of the sound. The nasalization of vowels in English generally follows after the initial articulation of the sound. We may say that French vowels are nasal, while English vowels are nasalized. Pairs such as the following bring out the contrast:

bond	/bɔnd/	/bõ/	bond	
blond	/blɔnd/	/blõ/	blond	MID, BACK, ROUNDED
uncle	/ʌnkl/	/õkl/	oncle	NASAL /õ/
dunk	/dʌnk/	/dõk/	donc	
grand	/grænd/	/grã/	grand	
tan	/tæn/	/tã/	tant	LOW, FRONT
band	/bænd/	/bãd/	bande	NASAL /ã/
land	/lænd/	/lãd/	lande	
sent	/sɛnt/	/sɛ̃t/	sainte	
meant	/mɛnt/	/mɛ̃t/	mainte	MID, FRONT
mince	/mɪns/	/mɛ̃s/	mince	NASAL /ɛ̃/
zinc	/zɪnk/	/zɛ̃k/	zinc	

We offer no examples of minimal pairs for /œ̃/, because in rapid, informal speech many speakers tend not to contrast /ɛ̃/ and /œ̃/, as in **brin** and **brun,** generally favoring /ɛ̃/. Hence we need not insist that students learn the sound /œ̃/ in the initial stage of their training.

English / German   The following are examples of bilingual pairs for the practice of phonemes which present problems for the learner of German.

A widely used German counterpart of our /r/ is a dorso-uvular fricative, almost like French /ʀ/. The instructions given earlier for the articulation of French /ʀ/ apply also for uvular German /ʀ/. To become aware of the contrast between American /r/ and German /ʀ/, the student might use pairs like **earnest** /ərnəst/ — **ernst** /ɛʀnst/. Still, German /ʀ/ is not a pressing phonological problem, and we need not spend precious time on practicing it at this level of learning.

For German umlauts, the explanation given for French /y/ and /œ/ applies. Pairs such as the following bring out the contrast between English /u/ and German /y/:

coon	/kuːn/	/kyn/	kühn
cool	/kuːl/	/kyl/	kühl	HIGH, CENTRAL,
boon	/buːn/	/bynə/	Bühne	ROUNDED /y/
mood	/muːd/	/mydə/	müde

The distinction between /y/, as in **müde,** and its shorter allophone, as in **müssen,** is generally nonfunctional and need not be brought up at this point. The sound /ø/, as in **König,** may be considered an allophone of /œ/, as in **können,** and will be discussed in the next chapter.

The phoneme /œ/ may be practiced in pairs such as these:

hall	/hɔl/	/hœlə/	Hölle
gotten	/gɔtn/	/gœtəʀ/	Götter	MID-LOWER
corner	/kɔənr/	/kœʀnəʀ/	Körner	CENTRAL /œ/
horn	/hɔrn/	/hœʀnəʀ/	Hörner

The final sound in **Hörner** is phonetically different from medial /ʀ/ in the same word. We will discuss this difference later and will give the so-called reduced final /ʀ/ a special phonetic symbol.

Experience also indicates that it is better to postpone practicing the sound symbolized [ç], which is an allophone of the fricative /x/ and comes to most students rather naturally after they have learned the phoneme /x/.

In German /x/, pronunciation may be helped by having the learner articulate successively a highly aspirated /k/ in *duck* and then gradually cease to make the occlusion for /k/, so that the terminal sound becomes a velar fricative, as in German **Dach.** Following are examples of possible pairs:

dock	/dɔk/	/dox/	doch	DORSO-VELAR
lock	/lɔk/	/lox/	Loch	(OR UVULAR)
knock	/nɔk/	/noch/	noch	UNVOICED FRICATIVE
cock	/kɔk/	/kox/	Koch	/x/ (Sketch 3)

The natural tendency of English speakers to substitute the sound /č/
for /x/ can be counteracted by pairs like the following, in which the
allophone [ç] is articulated quite naturally because of the ending of
the German words:

reach	/ri:č/	/ʀi:xə/	rieche
merchant	/mɛrčnt/	/mɛʀxən/	Märchen

Occasionally, students respond better to separated syllables:
Märchen /mɛʀ-xən/, **Mädchen** /met-xən/, **Gretchen** /gʀet-xən/.

Some speakers of American English do not have a vowel /ɔ/ accept-
ably close to the German vowel in **Gott.** If they pronounce *sought* as
/sat/, the German /o/ may have to be treated as a new phoneme and
practiced through contrastive pairs:

dock	/dak/	/dok/	Dock	
pock	/pak/	/pokə/	Pocke	
locked	/lakt/	/lokt/	lockt	MID, BACK, /o/
cost	/kast/	/kost/	Kost	

The next step can be the following pairs, provided the learner has a
good model and is able to round the vowel without adding a glide:

nought	/nat - nɔt/	/not/	Not
often	/afən - ɔfən/	/ofən/	Ofen
Austin	/astən - ɔstən/	/ostən/	Osten
taught	/tat - tɔt/	/tot/	Tot

English / Russian   The Russian consonant /x/ is acoustically
similar to its German counterpart. The learner may be asked to
articulate successively a highly aspirated /k/ as in *duke* and gradually remove the occlusion so that he ends up with a velar fricative
as the last sound in дух (spirit). In final position this consonant is not
as difficult as it is initially or medially. Hence practice should start
with one or two pairs in which the Russian word *ends* in /x/:

duke	/duk/	/dux/	дух	
Czech	/ček/	/čex/	чех	DORSO-VELAR,
mechanic	/məkænɪk/	/m̥ixáṇik/	механик	UNVOICED
caught	/kɔt/	/xot/	ход	FRICATIVE /x/
clef	/klef/	/x̣lef/	хлев	(Sketch 4)
could	/kʊd/	/xudój/	худой	

The problem of the palatalized Russian consonants cannot be pragmatically approached through English-Russian contrastive pairs. We do not have enough minimal pairs to contrast all English consonants with palatalized Russian counterparts. It is relatively easy, however, to find minimal pairs in Russian (monolingual pairs) for palatalized consonants as well as "soft" variants of vowels /a/, /o/, /u/, /ɨ/, and /e/.

The so called "hard" vowels do have acceptable counterparts in the English vocalic system. Those speakers, however, who do not distinguish between the vowel in *cot* and in *caught*, using /a/ in both, should be introduced to Russian /o/ as to a difficult phoneme.

To achieve the acoustic quality of this vowel, it is suggested that learners start from the familiar position for /a/ but with lips rounded as for the first part of the diphthong in **coat.** At the same time, the cheeks must be drawn inward, narrowing the oral cavity and contributing to the tense sound of the vowel. The following minimal pairs may be practiced for contrast:

cot	/kat/	/kót/ кот	
sock	/sak/	/sók/ сок	MID-HIGHER,
pot	/pat/	/pót/ пот	BACK, ROUNDED /o/
got	/gat/	/gót/ год	

English / Spanish   Some speakers of Spanish have an unvoiced fricative quite similar to the German or Russian /x/. It occurs as the initial sound in words such as **jefe** or **general.** By and large, this /x/ is limited to European speakers of Spanish. Spanish Americans generally use its voiced variant symbolized as /g̶/. This sound is comparable to the /h/ in **hay** although it is not a glottal. Instead, it is distinctly articulated by the dorsum constricting the air as it passes the uvula. Thus, its point of articulation is nearly the same as for the sound /g/, however the air passes through instead of being stopped. The difference between the English /g/ and the Spanish /g̶/ is revealed in contrastive pairs such as these:

legal	/ligl/	/leg̶al/	legal	DORSO-UVULAR,
dig	/dɪg/	/dig̶a/	diga	VOICED, FRICATIVE,
vigor	/vɪgər/	/vig̶oř/	vigor	/g̶/ (Sketch 4)
figure	/fɪgər/	/fig̶uřa/	figura	

The nonocclusive Spanish /ƀ/, as in **lobo,** is produced at the same
point of articulation as /b/. The lips, however, only partially ob-
struct the passage of air and do not effect the occlusion necessary for
/b/. The /ƀ/ is pronounced as air passes between the lips. The sound
may be contrasted with /b/ in the following pairs:

lobby /labɪ/	/loƀo/ lobo	
Debby /dɛbɪ/	/deƀe/ debe	BILABIAL, VOICED,
Bobby /babɪ/	/boƀo/ bobo	FRICATIVE /b/
a bath /əbæθ/	/aƀađ/ abad	

The tapped /ř/ and the trilled /rr/ differ in their points of articulation and in their acoustic effect from the English retroflex /r/. The
articulation of /ř/ is comparable to that of English /d/ in **shudder:**
the apex taps the alveolae. The acoustic effect of /rr/ is caused by
trilling the apex on the alveolar ridge. The completely different positions of the tongue for our retroflex /r/ and Spanish /rr/ can be
practiced in these pairs:

berry /bɛrɪ/	/berra/ berra	
bore /bɔr/	/borre/ borre	APICO-ALVEOLAR,
ray /rej/	/rrej/ rey	TRILLED /rr/
Perry /pɛrɪ/	/perro/ perro	

In most of Spain and in a few areas of Latin America, people use a
sound described as lamino-palatal and lateral. It may be symbolized
either /ll/ or /ļ/. This sound is similar to the Russian palatalized /ļ/
and equally difficult to imitate. Its nearest but still imperfect English
approximation is the cluster /lj/, as in **value** /vælju/. In much of the
Spanish speaking world, however, the /ļ/ is replaced by the semi-
consonant /j/ familiar to speakers of English. Hence, we need not
make a point of teaching the sound /ļ/ in Spanish.

The phoneme /ñ/ as in **año** or **niño** is a sound similar to the English
colloquial contraction of /n/ and /j/ as in **onion** or **canyon.** We can
accept the /nj/ cluster heard in **onion** as a substitute for the Spanish
/ñ/ provided it is articulated as a single sound, a palatalized nasal. A
few comparisons of the English and the Spanish sound may be
useful:

onion /ʌnjən/	/año/ año
pinion /pɪnjən/	/peña/ peña
canyon /kænjən/	/kaña/ caña

As a rule, excellent basic-level results are obtained by teaching problem phonemes through phonemic contrasts with English. Occasionally, it may be difficult to find a satisfactory number of bilingual minimal pairs. The task can be made easier by consulting a dictionary, although the vocabulary within a textbook is usually sufficient.

Monolingual Pairs   The other series of pairs, which may be called monolingual, consists of contrasting words in the foreign language alone. The earlier-mentioned criteria of minimal contrast should be observed, and only one phoneme, if possible, should account for the difference between the words of a pair.

In some instances, the foreign phoneme has a distinct allophone, which is used whenever a certain grouping of sounds occurs or when the phoneme occupies a certain position in an utterance. Thus, in Spanish the flap /r/ phoneme is replaced by a trilled allophone when, in formal speech, it happens to be the last sound of an utterance. In such cases, for the purposes of monolingual pairs, we can use one of two approaches.

The first is to ignore the allophones as irrelevant for a beginner. In the case of monolingual pairs, this means that we place within a given set of pairs a sequence of words which contain both allophones of the foreign phoneme. For example, if the sound is /ø/ as in the French **neutre,** we can treat it as being functionally the same as the sound /œ/ in **meurtre.** The same is true of the German umlauts /ø/ as in **König** and /œ/ as in **können.** If both sounds are allowed to occur in one side of the set of pairs, we are using the so-called phonemic approach.

The alternate approach is to provide two sets of pairs in each case. In one set, on the right side, we use only words which contain the first of the two allophones. In the other set, we use only words that contain the second allophone. (There can be more than two distinct allophones, but only two are normally relevant for teaching.) This procedure slows down the learning of the problem phonemes, but it teaches the student a more native pronunciation and aids him to realize the importance of complementary distribution. This may be called the allophonic approach.

French   The allophonic approach is exemplified by the introduction of /ø/ into the following series of minimal pairs. The reason for doing this is to demonstrate the French custom of using in open syllables an allophone that is distinctly different from that used in closed syllables. The former is symbolized as /ø/, the latter as /œ/.[1] While the articulation of /œ/ is characterized by lowering the lamina and relaxing the lips, the sound /ø/ is articulated with the lamina raised and the lips protruding and tensely rounded. The following pairs should be practiced, preferably with the aid of a native speaker:

/ɛ/	/œ/	/u/	/ø/
l'air	l'heure	ou	eux
père	peur	pou	peux
nef	neuf	fou	feu
gêne	jeune	doux	deux
sel	seul	goût	gueux

/i/	/y/	/u/	/y/
ire	hure	dessous	dessus
pire	pure	la roue	la rue
gris	grue	la cour	la cure
rit	rue	la mouette	la muette
vie	vue	une moule	une mule
dîne	dune	il l'avoue	il l'a vu

French nasal vowels may be learned through contrasts with their nonnasal counterparts or by contrast of one nasal vowel with another. The first approach includes pairs such as these:

/ɛ/	/ɛ̃/	/a/	/ã/
tes	teint	ta	tant
paix	pain	bas	ban
/o/	/õ/	cas	quand
tôt	ton	sa	sans
pot	pont	chat	chant

---

[1] In formal speech, /ø/ may occur in closed syllables, as it does in **pieuse, feutre, jeûne,** and the existence of the minimal pair **jeûne** /žøn/—**jeune** /žœn/ could give /ø/ and /œ/ the status of two phonemes. In this instance the two sounds are treated as allophones.

A special problem is the learner's tendency to nasalize any vowel preceding a nasal consonant. Occasionally, French does not permit such nasalization and the following pairs are worth practicing:

ancien	/ãsjɛ̃/	/ãsjɛn/	ancienne
le mien	/ləmjɛ̃/	/lamjɛn/	la mienne
bon	/bõ/	/bon/	bonne
ton	/tõ/	/ton/	tonne
Jean	/žã/	/žan/	Jeanne
banc	/bã/	/ban/	banne

The second approach includes the following pairs:

/ɛ̃/	/ã/	/õ/	/ã/
saint	sang	son	sans
teint	temps	ton	temps
gain	gant	qu'on	camp
lin	lent	plomb	plan
bain	banc	bon	banc
vin	vent	vont	vend

A confusion of the nasals /ɛ̃/ and /õ/ is not a problem. Students are not likely to need practice with pairs such as **saint — son** or **bain — bon.** On the other hand, the sounds /ɛ̃/ and /ã/ or /õ/ and /ã/ are more likely to be confused, partly because of a phono-semantic interference from English. For example, **temps** evokes the English word **tempest** /tɛmpəst/ and thus tends to be heard and mispronounced as /tɛ̃/. Similarly, **blond** can evoke the English **blond** /bland/ and may be heard and mispronounced as /blã/ with the consequent confusion of such words as **blond** /blõ/ and **blanc** /blã/.

German   In the following sample sets of minimal pairs, words containing different allophones of the same phoneme are not separated. (The allophones differ in length accompanied by tension.) In the purely phonemic approach, it is not necessary that the student pronounce one allophone of /y/ in, for example, **gebühren** and another in **würden.** Allophones of the umlaut in **hören** and **Hörner** are considered one functional sound symbolized /œ/. The same is true of allophones of the sound /x/. Our sets of pairs are designed solely to define the acoustic qualities of three phonemes not heard in

English: /y/, /œ/, and /x/. Their allophones will be treated in the next chapter:

/u/	/y/	/ɪ/	/y/
Kunst	Künste	Kiste	Küste
Zug	Züge	Stille	Stühle
Fuss	Füsse	sticke	Stücke
Bruder	Brüder	Kissen	küssen

/ɛ/	/œ/	/ɔ/	/œ/
kennen	können	konnte	könnte
fällig	völlig	Kopf	Köpfe
helle	Hölle	offen	Öfen
Mächte	möchte	Stock	Stöcke

/k/	/x/	/g/	/x/
Kino	China	Kragen	krachen
nackt	Nacht	Magen	machen
taugt	taucht	lagen	lachen
Magd	Macht	wagen	wachen

The distinction between long and short vowels usually constitutes a minor learning problem. For example, the vowel distinction in **Magd** and **Macht** is comparable to that of the English **march** /mɑːč/ and **much** /mʌč/. The distinction between **bieten** and **bitten** resembles the difference between the English **beaten** and **bitten.**

The vowels in **Weg** and **weg** happen to be in phonemic contrast, but this is rather rare. The distinction between long and short vowels is most often allophonic, nonfunctional.

The long /e/ in **Weg** is like the /e/ of the English diphthong /ej/ as in **way.** Thus, it is a sound which exists in English; the only problem is that it invariably occurs with a glide or as a diphthong.

Russian   Certain palatalized sounds represent phonemes which do not exist in the English sound system. Others can be heard in English but rarely occur in the same position as in Russian. For example, we sometimes hear acceptable approximations of Russian palatalized /ḍ/, /ḷ/, /ṇ/, and /ṭ/ in these words:

due /dju/
value /vælju/
vineyard /vɪnjərd/
costume /kastjum/

The palatalized quality of English /d/, /l/, /n/, and /t/ is brought about by their assimilation to the neighboring semivowel /j/.

An approximation of the palatal sound /šč/ as in ещё occurs in the rapid sequence of /š/ and /č/ when we say **fresh cheese** or **cash checks.**

Phonemically significant contrasts between the Russian /d/ — /ḍ/, /l/ — /ļ/, /n/ — /ṇ/, and /t/ — /ṭ/ can be detected in these pairs:

и дом	/idom/	/iḍom/	идём
пыл	/pɨl/	/pɨļ/	пыль
нос	/nos/	/ṇos/	нёс
вид	/ɣit/	/ɣiṭ/	вить

Palatalization means a shift in the point of articulation, so that the palatalized sound is articulated closer to the point of articulation for the sound /j/. The production of an audible glide — as the shift takes place — is to be avoided.

Palatalizing /e/ in stressed positions before palatalized consonants can be approximated by the diphthong in **lay** /lej/, provided it is noticeably shortened. Examples: лень /ļeṇ/, дети /ḍéṭi/.

Phonemically significant contrasts between plain and palatalized consonant-vowel clusters also can be heard in the following pairs:

был	/bɨl/	/ḅil/	бил
быть	/bɨṭ/	/ḅiṭ/	бить
выл	/vɨl/	/ɣil/	вил
пыл	/pɨl/	/ṗil/	пил
лук	/luk/	/ḷuk/	люк

Spanish   Within the Spanish sound system, /đ/, /ƀ/, and /g/ are allophones of /d/, /b/, and /g/, respectively. They are in complementary distribution, occurring consistently in certain acoustic surroundings.

The nonocclusive allophone of /d/ is comparable to the English phoneme /đ/ as in **though** /đou/ and is a familiar sound to speakers of English. The Spanish /đ/ appears in any position except after /n/ and /l/ in a string of sounds. Hence, it does not occur in words like **mandar** or **falda.** It must be replaced by plain /d/ when it begins a string of sounds after a pause in speaking. Compare the following:

¿Dónde está? /donde/   Veo dónde está /beođonde/

The sound /ƀ/ occurs in any position except after /m/, as in **emblema** and after a pause in speaking. A word like **vino** starts with a /b/ if pronounced (by a careful speaker) as the first of a string of words. If, however, it is within an utterance and follows a vowel, it starts with the sound /ƀ/. Similarly, the sound /ǥ/ is used after vowels within an utterance but not after a pause in speaking. Contrastive pairs, such as the following, reveal the use of these problem sounds:

/b/	/ƀ/	/b/	/ƀ/
bía	íba	beso	este beso
béca	cabo	vaca	mi vaca
bóto	tubo	vino	su vino

/g/	/ǥ/	/g/	/ǥ/
gato	toga	gato	este gato
guía	oigo	guía	buena guía
gusto	augusto	gusto	mucho gusto

Tapped /ř/ and trilled /rr/ are two contrasting phonemes within the Spanish sound system. The latter is used after and before a pause in speaking and after /n/ as in **honra** /onrra/. Occasionally, it occurs in the middle of a word and signals a semantic contrast:

/ř/	/rr/
pero	perro
caro	carro
para	parra
coro	corro
fiero	fierro
foro	forro

Spanish vowels may be said to have passable substitutes in their nondiphthongized English counterparts. Thus, Spanish /a/, in general, is phonemically the same as the vowel in **lark,** or **start.** The Spanish /e/ of **beso** can be approximated with the slightly lengthened English vowel in **Ed** or **best.** The /o/ of **beso** is comparable to a somewhat shortened "aw" in **see-saw.** The /i/ of **mi** is quite close to the English vowel in **meek,** and the /u/ of **uno** is virtually the same phoneme heard in the English word **ooze.**

Phonemically, Spanish vowels are not terra incognita to speakers of English, although they do present certain problems on the phonetic level.

This chapter has dealt primarily with sounds absent from the English phonemic system. Some of the palatalized sounds of Russian, however, were not included, since they have been treated as allophones of the corresponding plain sounds. Our goal thus far has been significant functional sounds for which the student must develop "a new ear" and a new articulatory skill. Facial sketches, such as those presented in this chapter, can be helpful in showing students the position of the tongue and the lips.

TESTING AUDITORY DISCRIMINATION OF PHONEMES

The teacher selects about twenty model words, each of which contains a single problem phoneme. Next, he finds for each model a set of three words, only one of which contains the particular phoneme for which the model was selected. The other two words of the triplet differ from the model and from the one "right" word by only one or two sounds that are acoustically similar yet not identical with the problem (tested) phoneme.

During the test, each model word is repeated twice by the teacher (or recording) and followed in reasonably spaced succession by the first, second, and third word of the triplet. The students have about five seconds to identify by a letter (a, b, or c) the one word in the triplet which contains the problem phoneme. For example, in Spanish, the first model word may be **perro,** containing the problem phoneme /rr/. The test proceeds as follows:

(Model)   1. /perro/, /perro/
(Triplet)   a. /pero/   b. /ferro/   c. /sero/

The student who has discerned correctly will have written the letter
b next to number 1 on the answer sheet.

Several variations of this test may be developed for any foreign language. Instead of single words, the test may consist of pairs of meaningful utterances not exceeding seven syllables. The student first
hears a model word containing the problem sound, for example,
French /õ/ or /y/, as in **bon** or **a vu.** (The model may be given once
by a man's voice and once by a woman's voice.) Next, he hears the
first sentence twice and immediately determines if it contains the
model word. He marks "yes" or "no" (next to number 1) on the
answer sheet. Next he hears the second sentence twice and determines if it contains the model word. (One, both, or neither of the
pairs of sentences may contain the word.) Subsequently, the teacher
(or recording) supplies the next model and the students listen in the
same manner for two similar sentences and mark their choice. Here
is an example of this type of test in French:

> /bõ/   (twice)
> 1. C'est beau comme ça?   (twice)
> 2. C'est bon comme ça?   (twice)
>
> /a vy/   (twice)
> 3. Il l'a vu?   (twice)
> 4. Il l'avoue?   (twice)

Correct answers are "no" for 1 and 4, and "yes" for 2 and 3.

The sentence pairs are set up on the principle of phonemic contrasts,
such as French nasal versus oral articulation (**bon — beau, orange
— orage**), central versus back articulation (**a vu — avoue, la rue —
la roue**), or voicing as against unvoicing of consonants (**base —
basse, ils ont — ils sont**). Tense and lax vowels may also be contrasted, as in German **bieten — bitten,** or plain versus palatalized
consonants, as in Russian **бил — был.**

Supplementary Reading

Archibald A. Hill, "Language Analysis and Language Teaching," reprinted
in *Foreign Language Teaching. An Anthology,* (New York: Macmillan,
1967) pp. 91–111.

Norman P. Sacks, "Some Aspects of the Application of Linguistics to the Teaching of Modern Foreign Languages," *Modern Language Journal,* XLVIII (January, 1964): pp. 7–17.

Hilario S. Peña, "Practical Linguistics for the FLES Teacher," in *Readings in Foreign Languages for the Elementary School* (Waltham, Mass., 1967), pp. 221–224.

Mary Finocchiaro, *Teaching Children Foreign Languages* (New York: McGraw-Hill, 1964), Chapters 4, 5, and 6.

Fred M. Chreist, *Foreign Accent,* (Englewood Cliffs, N.J.: Prentice-Hall, 1964), Chapters 3 and 6.

6 PRACTICAL HINTS: PHONETICS

PHONETIC DIFFERENCES

This chapter deals with allophones and learning problems of a phonetic nature. As we have already observed, phonemes are affected by the company they keep. The normally unvoiced /t/ in **pitty** is so acted upon by the voiced neighbors on both sides that it becomes almost a /d/.

If a learner of American English desires to reach near native pronunciation, he will have to respect the phonetic difference between the /t/ he has learned in words like **tea** or **tap** and the kind of /t/ we commonly use in **pitty** or **butter.** Conversely, when we are the learners, we have to adjust to the fickleness of the foreign language phonemes.

In the area of phonemic differences, the student had to learn new functional sounds; in the area of phonetics, he is merely learning to acquire a better, more native pronunciation. As he procedes, he must bear in mind that phonetic or subphonemic differences do not normally change meaning but are frequently one of the reasons for an accent.

FRENCH

Consonants   One characteristic of French consonants is energetic articulation, requiring a greater effort than that needed for the articulation of consonants in English. This energetic articulation makes for clarity and firmness, particularly in the last syllable. Compare, for example, the lax English apico-alveolar /l/, as in **the table,** and the tense French apico-dental /l/, as in **la table.** The fact that the French final /l/ is somewhat unvoiced does not reduce its tenseness. This apico-dental variant of /l/ occurs also in English before the sound /θ/, as in **health** /hɛlθ/. Similarly, compare the lax English alveolar /s/ in **mercy** with the tense, energetic, dental /s/ in French **merci.**

The dorso-uvular vibrant, symbolized /ʀ/, is typical of middle-class educated speech, the "accepted" speech of the land. Its articulation has already been described and is depicted in facial sketch 3 in the preceding chapter. To produce this particular sound, the student should pretend to gently gargle without causing excessive turbulance of air in the uvula. Some students find it easier to articulate the tapped apico-alveolar variant common to many parts of the French-speaking world.

The French consonantal system does not have the affricates /č/ and /ǰ/. English-speaking students of French should be careful not to pronounce words like **charité** with an initial /č/ or **journal** with an initial /ǰ/. The tendency to use /č/ or /ǰ/ instead of French /ž/ in final position in words such as **range** and **grange** must also be avoided. Contrastive pairs, such as the following, are useful with the reminder that all syllables in French are evenly stressed:

	ENGLISH		FRENCH
jolly	/ǰɔlɪ/	/žoli/	joli
jest	/ǰest/	/žest/	geste
gymnast	/ǰɪmnæst/	/žimnast/	gymnaste
genital	/ǰenɪtl/	/ženital/	génital
garage	/gʌrɑǰ/	/garaž/	garage
mirage	/mɪrɑǰ/	/miraž/	mirage

The aspiration typical of English /p/, /t/, and /k/ in initial prevocalic positions is nonexistent in French. For example, the /p/ of **père** is no different from the /p/ of **prêt.** The following pairs present a sample of a useful drill:

	ENGLISH		FRENCH
cause	/kʰɔz/	/koz/	cause
pool	/pʰul/	/pul/	poule
tear	/tʰɛr/	/tɛʀ/	taire

pair	/pʰɛr/	/pɛʀ/ père
car	/kʰɑr/	/kaʀ/ car
tall	/tʰɔl/	/tol/ tôle

Because of the articulatory-economy habits of English speakers, the sound /s/, when followed by /j/, is frequently pronounced as /š/. Examples: **This year** /ɗɪšjiːr/, **is your** /ɪšjər/. Beginning students are apt to hear and pronounce **monsieur** as /məšɜ/. Such economy habit must not be allowed in French, where the sequence /sj/ and /šj/ can occasionally be phonemically contrasting; example: **C'est le sien** and **c'est le chien.**

We must also guard against confusing /sj/ with /š/ in words such as **décoration** and **diction.** Bilingual pairs are easy to prepare and should be used to drill the distinction. Some consideration should be given to difficulty with the sequence /zj/, as in the French **dérision** or **vision.** Students are likely to confuse /zj/ with /ž/, since the former is not a common sound cluster in English. The following pairs are suggested for drill:

ENGLISH		FRENCH	
vision	/vɪžn/	/vizjõ/	vision
precision	/prɛsɪžn/	/prɛsizjõ/	précision
occlusion	/ɔklužn/	/oklyzjõ/	occlusion
fusion	/fjužn/	/fyzjõ/	fusion

Another common error occurs in the sequence /ps/, which students are likely to replace with /s/ in words beginning with **psych-** or **pseudo-.** Again, bilingual pairs are easy to find. The sounds /t/ and /d/ are distinctly apico-dental and comparable to English variants used before /θ/ as in **eighth** and **width.**

Vowels From a phonetic point of view, none of the French vocalic sounds are articulated in exactly the same way as their English counterparts. The unusual tenseness of French vowels is physically noticeable in the position of the lips. A French speaker, pronouncing his back vowels, rounds and moves his lips much further forward than an English speaker. On the other hand, in pronouncing the front vowels, he spreads his lips into sharp corners as if to smile. An exception is the vowel /ɛ/, as in **prêt,** which is articulated with semirounded lips.

Correct articulation of French vowels requires greater articulatory effort than in English. Unless a learner of French feels that extra exertion needed to achieve vocalic tenseness, his vowels are apt to be too lax. The greatest articulatory effort is probably required for the production of French /y/. (Its articulation is shown in sketch 1, page 117.) As a supplement to the bilingual and monolingual pairs suggested for the practice of /y/ in the preceding chapter, a combination of vowel and pitch practice such as the following is suggested:

Où vas-tu?	Il est perdu?
Entendu?	Tu l'as vu?
C'est la rue?	Vous l'avez lu?

It has been found that some students grasp the true acoustic quality of /y/ only when they hear and pronounce it as the last sound in an utterance with a rising pitch contour.

To appreciate the tenseness of French /o/ as opposed to English /ɔ/, contrast the following and use the device of rising-falling intonation to bring out the quality of /o/:

ENGLISH /ɔ/	FRENCH /o/
dolphin	Quel dauphin?
maul	Quel môle?
caught	Quelle côte?
bought	Quelle beauté?

The tenseness of the French /o/ and of other vocalic sounds can vary, however. Most tense vowels have a lax variant, which in some cases acquires the status of a phoneme.

In colloquial speech, tense vowels occur in open syllables and lax vowels in closed syllables. An exception to this broad rule is the long, tense /o/ in closed syllables before /z/, as in **chose** /šo:z/ or **pause** /po:z/. Other exceptions are monosyllabic words ending in a consonant preceded by **au,** as in **fausse,** or circumflex **ô,** as in **hôte.**

Similarly, a tense /ø/, normally occurring in open syllables, may occur in closed syllables before /z/, as in **creuse** /kʀøz/, and in words such as **jeûne,** where the vowel is spelled with a circumflex.

The following sets of pairs may be used to practice the distinction between tense and lax vowels in open and closed syllables:

/e/	/ɛ/	/o/	/ɔ/
nez	neige	sot	sotte
thé	tête	dos	dot /dɔt/
pied	pièce	veau	vote
ces	cette	lot	lotte

/ø/	/œ/
peu	peur
eux	heure
ceux	seuil
deux	deuil
feux	feuille
il peut	ils peuvent

In formal speech, French /ɛ/ occurs in open syllables, and speakers who are proud of their pronunciation contrast it with /e/.

The tense /o/, in guarded speech, occasionally occurs in closed syllables and is used as functional contrast.

The following are examples of formal contrast between open-syllabic /e/ and /ɛ/ and between closed-syllabic /o/ and /ɔ/:

/e/	/ɛ/	/o/	/ɔ/
fée	fait	paume	pomme
les	lait	saute	sotte
des	dès	ôte	hotte
j'ai	j'aie	côte	cote
j'aurai	j'aurais	vôtre	votre

The tense, frontal /a/ has a variant used only by careful speakers of the language to indicate a functional contrast:

/a/	/ɑ/
battons	bâton
patte	pâte
bal	Bâle
mal	mâle
tache	tâche
ta	tas
la	las
ma	mât

Many speakers fail to distinguish between /a/ and /ɑ/. Schane claims[1] that, because of the unstable character of the vowel **a**, its two variants may be considered as a stylistic phenomenon in modern French and not as two sounds representing a "true" phonemic contrast. In our simplified transcription, we employ a single symbol /a/ to represent both variants of the vowel.

With respect to nasal vowels, phoneticians recognize four sounds: /ã/, /õ/, /ɛ̃/, and /œ̃/. Few speakers, however, consistently distinguish between /ɛ̃/ and /œ̃/, and many use only /ɛ̃/. For example, **un ingénieur** is pronounced either /œ̃nɛ̃ženjœʀ/ or /ɛ̃nɛ̃ženjœʀ/.[2]

Examine, however, the following contrastive pairs in which a distinction persists:

brin /bʀɛ̃/   /bʀœ̃/ brun
ainsi /ɛ̃si/   /œ̃si/ un si ...

Lastly, let us consider the French semivowel /w/ and its significant allophone symbolized [ɥ]. The semivowel is a shortened /w/ and may be phonetically symbolized as [u̯]. It occurs in words like **ouest, oui, Louis** and differs phonetically from the English semivowel /w/, as in **west.** For the English sound, the tongue stays down, as it would for the articulation of /b/ or /v/. For the French sound, the dorsum is raised considerably toward the velum, as for the articulation of the first sound in **ouvrir.** The phonetic contrast can be practiced in the following pairs:

ENGLISH /w/	FRENCH /w/ OR [u̯]
west	ouest
was	oiseau
Dwight	doigt
watt	ouate

The semivocalic sound symbolized [ɥ] occurs in words such as **huit, juin, lui, conduire.** While the dorsum is raised toward the velum

---

[1] Sanford A. Schane, *French Phonology and Morphology* (Cambridge, Massachusetts: M.I.T. Press, 1968) p. 19.
[2] See Albert Valdman, "Phonologic Structure and Social Factors in French: the Vowel 'un'," *The French Review*, XXXIII (Dec. 1959): 153–161.

in articulating /w/, it is raised closer to the center of the palate in articulating [ɥ]. Pairs like the following will help the student recognize the phonetic difference between /w/ and [ɥ]:

FRENCH /w/	FRENCH [ɥ]
Louis	lui
louer	lueur
joint	juin
oui	huile

The glide [ɥ], which occurs whenever an /y/ is followed by another vowel, may also be studied in pairs:

tue /ty/	tuer /tɥe/
pus /py/	puer /pɥe/

GERMAN

Consonants   There is a marked difference between the use of English and German voiced consonants. In German, consonants in word-final position are unvoiced. Observe, for example, the morphophonemic change from **grobe** /grobə/ to **grob** /grop/, from **Tage** /tagə/ to **Tag** /tak/, and from **Wände** /vɛndə/ to **Wand** /vant/. The sounds /b/, /g/, and /d/ become /p/, /k/, and /t/, respectively.

Many consonants in initial position are semivoiced. **Danke** and **bitte,** for example, begin with sounds rather close to the unvoiced consonants /t/ and /p/. In phonetic transcription, this partial unvoicing may be marked by a subliteral diacritic, as in [d̥ankə] and [b̥ɪtə].

The consonant /r/ as in **rot** or **beraten** is pronounced either as an apico-alveolar tap or as a dorso-velar or dorso-uvular fricative. The tapped variant is similar to the Russian and the Spanish sounds symbolized by /r̃/. The velar or uvular sound is phonetically symbolized by [ʀ]. The latter resembles the French "correct" variant of /r/ and is articulated in the same manner: the tip of the tongue leans on the lower teeth, while the dorsum is raised to constrict the air (see sketch 1, page 117).

In order to clarify the difference in the point of articulation for our retroflex /r/ and the German /r̆/ or /ʀ/, pairs such as these may be practiced:

ENGLISH /r/	GERMAN /r̆/ or /ʀ/
radio	Radio
room	Ruhm
rot	Rat

In final position, German /r/ is reduced to a semivocalic sound much like the final sound in **sofa.** The phonetic symbol for this sound is either [ʀ] or [ʌ]. The latter symbol is preferable and may be used in a modified phonemic transcription: **Wasser** [vasʌ], **Messer** [mɛsʌ], **wer** [veʌ].

German /t/, as in **Vater, Butter,** is not partially voiced, as it often is in the articulation of English **water** or **butter.** German speakers retain the aspiration in medially positioned /t/.

A noticeable phonetic difference exists between German and English /l/. While English /l/, in final position, is often articulated with the apex or the lamina remaining in touch with the palate. German /l/ is produced by the apex making a quick contact with the alveolar ridge or the upper teeth. This difference may be clarified through contrastive pairs:

ENGLISH /l/	GERMAN [l]
pill	Pille
fell	Fell
hell	hell

The sound /s/ is substandard in the initial prevocalic position of native German words. **Sagen** is pronounced /zagən/, **singen** /ziŋgən/, etc. In preconsonantal positions, **s** is pronounced /š/, with the exception of a few northern dialects. In words of nonnative stock, however, the sound /s/ is standard in initial position: **Skizze** /skicə/, **Sphäre** /sfɛrə/, **Szene** /scenə/.

The sound /c/, also symbolized /ts/, is heard in words like **ziehen, zehn, Zimmer.** In English, it is initially heard in rare words like **tsetse fly** but quite often in medial and final positions of words like **announcement** /ənauncmɛnt/ or **bits.** Students not accustomed to using it initially tend to substitute the consonant /z/. This may represent a significant phonemic error, since the meaning of certain words depends on the contrast between /c/ and /z/:

Zahl /ca:l/	Saal /za:l/
Zoll /col/	soll /zol/
zehn /ce:n/	sehen /ze:n/

Practice is needed only for /c/ in initial position. An acceptable substitute is the /ts/ of **tsar,** provided the two consonants are articulated rapidly enough to produce the acoustic effect of a single sound. Pairs such as these are useful:

ENGLISH /z/	GERMAN /c/
zinc	Zink
zebra	Zebra
zelot	Zelot

The sound /x/, on the phonetic level, has two variants. After front vowels, after the sound /l/, and in the ending **-chen,** it becomes a palatal fricative symbolized [ç]: **sich** /ziç/, **König** /køniç/, **Milch** /milç/, **Märchen** /mɛrçən/. In all other positions, the sound is a velar fricative: **auch** /aux/ and **wachen** /vaxən/. The phonetic difference is audible in the following pairs:

/x/	[ç]
doch	dich
mach	mich
gewacht	Gewicht
gedacht	Gedicht

Consonantal sound clusters such as /št/ in **stehen,** /šn/ in **Schnee,** or /šp/ in **spielen** are relatively easy to mimic. More difficult are those in which one of the constituent sounds does not commonly occur in English, particularly the combinations /xt/ (or/çt/), /xc/ (or [çc]), and /xst/ (or /çst/).

The more difficult consonant clusters should be practiced in contrastive pairs, such as these:

/xt/ ([çt])	/xc/ ([çc])	/xt/ ([çt)]	/xst/ ([çst)]
Nacht	nachts	macht	machst
nicht	nichts	lacht	lachst
recht	rechts	braucht	brauchst
Rücksicht	rücksichtslos	bricht	brichst

Vowels   Certain vocalic sounds differ not only in quantity, as they do in English, but also in quality.[1] Some German vowels have not only a short and a long variant but also a tense and a lax variant. The diacritic indicating length is a colon, and the diacritic indicating tenseness is a dot placed under the vowel symbol. Thus, the acoustic contrast between **Staat** and **Stadt** is phonetically marked [štạːt] and [štạt]. Moulton uses this marking in his *The Sounds of English and German.* Our modified system of transcription obviates subliteral diactritics for German. The tense, long   wel in **Staat** can be transcribed by the symbol [ɑ]. Occasionally, a   ion is added to indicate length. The phonetic symbol [a] then re   sents a lax variant, relatively shorter in stressed syllables. Similarˌ , the symbol [e] may be used for the vowel in **Weg** and the symbol [ɛ] for its lax and short variant in **weg** (away).

In general, stressed, tense vowels are long; lax vowels are somewhat shorter. Only unstressed tense and unstressed lax vowels may be of equal duration. The following contrastive pairs are useful in distinguishing [ɑ] from [a] and [ɛ] from [e]:

/ɑ/	/a/	/e/	/ɛ/
Staat	statt	stehen	stechen
Saat	satt	Besen	Becken
Bahn	Bann	beten	Betten
kam	Kamm	stehlen	stellen
haben	hatten	Weg	weg

The distinction between tense and lax vowels and their duration is normally supported by stress. Thus, in **viel** [fiːl] the primary syllabic stress entails tenseness and length of the vowel, whereas the weak stress on the same vowel in **vielleicht** [fiːlajçt] allows a relaxation of [iː]. Relaxation of the long vowel tends to shorten it, so that most speakers will automatically say [fɪlajçt]. The symbol [ɪ] may be used for the lax variant of /i/. The lax vowel in a word like **spät,** however, is always long. This exception to the general rule includes words with vowel **ä** as in **Käse** [kɛːzə] and **Mädchen** [mɛːtçən]. Some speakers

------

[1]Vocalic quantity in English is shown by the differing length of the vowel in, for example, **sat** (short) and **sad** (longer).

of English use this variant of the vowel in words like **men, beds, eggs.**

The tenseness of German /i:/ may be practiced through bilingual contrastive pairs, making the student aware of the difference between the lax English vowel in, for example, **eagle** and its tense counterpart in German **ihn** /i:n/. German vowels are articulated with the lamina raised closer to the palate. English vowels are characterized by an upglide:

ENGLISH [ij]	GERMAN [i:]
bean	Biene
beaten	bieten
fee	Vieh

To differentiate German /ɪ/ from its long, tense variant, the following sample pairs are useful:

[ɪ]	[i:]
in	ihn
binnen	Bienen
Mitte	Miete
Minne	Miene
Schiff	schief

There are very few words in which the substitution of the sound /y/ by its variant [y:], or the replacement of /œ/ by /ø/, causes a change in meaning. Nevertheless, the phonetic difference between variants of the two sounds exists, and students of the language should develop a feeling for the use of /y/ as against /y:/ and of /œ/ as against /ø/. The following contrastive pairs show both sounds with their tense variants in stressed position, which adds length to tenseness:

/y/	/y:/	/œ/	/ø:/
Dürre	Düse	östlich	Österreich
mürbe	müde	könnt	tönt
würden	Süden	könne	Söhne
Kürze	kühne	dörre	höre
Hütte	Hüte	öffnen	Öfen

RUSSIAN

Consonants   In Russian, as in German, voiced consonants are unvoiced when they occur in final position. Although only voiced consonants are heard in any inflected form of a word like **год** (year), its uninflected form ends in a sound which is more /t/ than /d/. Unlike German and English, Russian prevocalic stops are not aspirated. A set of bilingual contrastive pairs may be used to teach students not to aspirate Russian /p/, /t/, /k/:

pot	/pʰɔt/	пот	/pot/
tourist	/tʰurɪst/	турист	/turíst/
coffee	/kʰɔfɪ/	кофе	/kófə/

The sound /l/ is articulated in two ways, both different from English articulation. The plain, "hard" Russian /l/ has its nearest English equivalent in the final sound of **pull.** When producing the Russian /l/, the apex leans on the base of the upper teeth or the alveolar ridge, the lamina is lowered, but the dorsum is raised in the area of the velum. The hollow thus formed between the surface of the tongue and the palate is greater than when articulating /l/ of **pull.** The increased cavity gives the Russian /l/ its peculiarly deep "hard" tone. Students may have some difficulty imitating the sound when it occurs in an initial position:

лоб,   лóдка,   лáдно,   лунá,   лы́жи

The palatalized variant of Russian /l/, symbolized /ļ/, is articulated differently. The apex, instead of touching the alveolar ridge, leans forward and heavily against it, while the rest of the tongue is raised toward the palate. The decreased cavity between the surface of the tongue and the palate gives /ļ/ a tone reminiscent of English /l/ in **value:**

лев,   лифт,   любóвь,   нельзя́,   полёт,   пóле,   пыль,   кремль

Russian /r/ also has two articulations, both different from English. English /r/ is usually an apical retroflex toward the postalveolar area, without actual contact and without vibration. The plain Russian /r/, symbolized /ř/, is an apico-alveolar trill. This means that the apex taps the alveolar ridge, sometimes more than once, but very rapidly:

рад, рот, рóза, рукá, ромáн, рубéж, фрáза, вéра

Palatalized /ŗ/ differs in that it is articulated with the entire tongue raised toward the palate, while the apex vibrates at the alveolar ridge. The cavity between tongue and palate is considerably smaller:

рис, рёв, речь, пря́мо, грех, словáрь, зверь

Palatalized alveolar stops /ţ/ and /ḑ/ are characterized by a considerable leaning of the lamina on the postalveolar palate, followed by a plosive sound (not identical with aspiration), which may be heard as a friction:

тень, тéшить, теплó, тепéрь,
день, дéло, дéти, дя́дя

Palatalized /ņ/ is comparable to the English nasal in **onion,** except that the lamina in Russian leans on the alveolar ridge rather than the palate:

нет, ня́ня, никáк, никтó, тень, óчень.

The velar stops /k/ and /g/ are palatalized by moving the constriction of air from the velum to the front palate, accompanied by a narrowing of the space between the lips. There is also a certain amount of audible friction of the released air. This friction is not aspiration as we know it in English:

кивáть, кúслый, гид, герóй, кем,
кéпка, гéний, гипс

The articulation of palatalized bilabials /ḅ/, /p̣/, /ṃ/ involves a forward movement of the tongue concurrent with the closure of the lips. Because of the new position of the tongue, the released sound is then marked with the acoustic quality of /j/ as in **yes:**

без, бил, бич, пя́тка,
пирóг, мёд, медь, мир

In the palatalized fricatives /f̣/, /ṿ/, /ṣ/, /z̧/, the passage of air is generally more constricted than for the production of their non-palatalized counterparts — natural result of moving the tongue up and forward toward the palate:

фильм,   фина́л,   вес,   век,
    семь,   сюда́,   зима́,   зе́лень

The palatalization of the sound symbolized /x/ is effected by raising the dorsum considerably toward the area where the velum meets the palate. This entails a slight withdrawal of the rest of the tongue and a narrowing of the bilabial opening. The student should start by producing /j/ as in **yield** and then unvoice it. The transition from voiced to unvoiced is necessarily quick, and only the unvoiced sound is kept. The unvoiced sound is Russian /x̣/, heard initially in words like **химия** and **хитрый**.

The following sample sets of contrastive pairs may be supplemented by other sets for practicing pronunciation of palatalized consonants:

/b/		/ḅ/	
был	/bɨl/	бил	/ḅil/
быт	/bɨt/	бить	/ḅiṭ/

/v/		/ɣ/	
воз	/vos/	вёз	/ɣos/
выл	/vɨl/	вил	/ɣil/

/g/		/g̣/	
гул	/gul/	гид	/git/
гусь	/guṣ/	гипс	/g̣ips/

/k/		/ḳ/	
кот	/kot/	кит	/ḳit/
купе	/kupe	кепка	/ḳepkə/

/l/		/ḷ/	
лупа	/lupə/	липа	/ḷipə/
пыл	/pɨl/	пыль	/pɨḷ/

/m/		/ṃ/	
мыло	/mɨla/	мило	/ṃila/
матч	/mač/	мяч	/ṃač/

/n/		/ṇ/	
нос	/nos/	нёс	/ṇos/
дан	/dan/	дань	/daṇ/

/p/		/p̦/	
пыл	/pɨl/	пил	/p̦il/
пот	/pot/	печь	/p̦eč/
/r/		**/r̦/**	
рой	/roj/	рёв	/r̦of/
театр	/tiatr/	теперь	/tiper̦/
/s/		**/ș/**	
сад	/sat/	сять	/șaț/
судья	/sudjá/	сюда	/șudá/
/t/		**/ț/**	
ток	/tok/	тёк	/țok/
быт	/bɨt/	быть	/bɨț/
/x/		**/x̦/**	
хор	/xor/	химик	/x̦ímik/
хуже	/xyžə	хижина	/x̦ížinə/

Vowels In Russian, unlike German, the distinction between short and long vowels is subphonemic, nonfunctional. Lengthening a vowel has only emotional value.

The vowel symbolized /ɨ/ is phonetically different from the English /ɪ/ in **pill**. In articulating /ɨ/, as in **пыл** /pɨl/ (fervor), the lamina is raised in the form of a hunch toward the velum, the apex is withdrawn, and the lips are spread slightly more than for the English /ɪ/. The following pairs serve to demonstrate the difference:

sip	/sɪp/	сыпь	/sɨp̦/
sinn	/sɪn/	сын	/sɨn/
dim	/dɪm/	дым	/dɨm/
mill	/mɪl/	мыл	/mɨl/
bit	/bɪt/	быт	/bɨt/

In stressed syllables, Russian vowels have a distinct tenseness. The /a/ in **как** /kak/ is tenser and somewhat lower than the mid-western /a/ in **cock** /kak/. In phonetic transcription, the symbol [ɑ] is used to designate the Russian sound. These pairs serve to emphasize the contrast:

sod	/sad/	сад	[sɑt]
mock	/mak/	мак	[mɑk]

mom /mam/   мама [mɑmə]
cock /kak/   как [kɑk]

The tense Russian /o/ should be clearly contrasted with the lax English /ɔ/:

wrought /rɔt/   рот   /rot/
sought /sɔt/   сотня /sótṇə/
bought /bɔt/   борт   /bort/
coffee   /kɔfɪ/   кофе /kófə/

In unstressed syllables, Russian vowels are subject to considerable modification by surrounding consonants. Thus, as part of an unstressed open syllable, the vowels represented by **"o"** and **"a"** become a sound resembling the English vowel in **but** /bʌt/; for example, **вода** is pronounced /vʌdá/, **жара** /žʌrá/.

The alternation of vocalic values in stressed and unstressed syllables presents a learning problem. It can be overcome by practicing contrastive pairs such as these:

/ó/		/ʌ/	
хóчещь	/xóčɪš/	хочý	/xʌčú/
пóезд	/pójəst/	поéздка	/pʌjéstkə/
пóсле	/pósḷə/	посóл	/pʌsól/
бóльше	/bólšə/	большóй	/bʌḷšój/
бóльно	/bólna/	болнóй	/bʌḷnój/
кóнчить	/kónčɪṭ/	кончáть	/kʌnčáṭ/

If the following syllable is also unstressed, the vocalic sound of the letter "o" resembles the first English vowel in **beret. Сторона,** for example, is pronounced /stərʌná/, **хорошо** /xərʌšó/. The same sound may be heard in the endings of the infinitive: **делать** /ḍélət/, **думать** /dúməṭ/.

After palatalized consonants, in an unstressed syllable, the vowel **"e"** or **"я"** is similar to the sound /i/: **несу** /ṇisú/, **деревня** /ḍiŗévṇə/, **пятнадцать** /pitnácəṭ/, **пятилетка** /piṭiḷétkə/.

In initial position, as an unstressed syllable, the vowel **"e"** or **"я"** is pronounced /ji/: **его** /jivó/, **её** /jijó/, **язык** /jizɪk/.

SPANISH

Consonants   In Spanish, as in French, no aspiration accompanies the release of air with /p/, /t/, and /k/. Contrastive bilingual pairs help students to discriminate between aspirated and unaspirated consonants:

ENGLISH	SPANISH
Peter [pʰiːtə]	Pedro /pedro/
tome [tʰoum]	tomo /tomo/
cart [kʰɑət]	carta /karta/
color [kʰʌlə]	color /kolor/

The Spanish system presents pronunciation problems with its two sounds of /r/, the nonocclusive /b̶/, /g̶/, /x/, /d̶/, and Castillian /ļ/.

The standard Spanish /ř/ is an apico-alveolar tap. The tongue apex taps the alveolar ridge in passing to the articulation of the next sound: **cero** /seřo/, **color** /koloř/, **gordo** /gořdo/. If the /ř/ is followed by another consonant, as in **gordo, porque, hermano,** there may be an audible, short trill (two quick, voiceless flaps). A distinctly trilled variant, symbolized /rr/, is required for the beginning of words and after /n/: **rueda** /rrued̶a/, **rey** /rrej/, **honra** /onrra/. Use of the tap as opposed to the trill can be phonemically significant, as in the following pair: **pero** /pero/ — **perro** /perro/.

The nonocclusive /d̶/ is comparable to the initial sound in **though.** Phonetically, however, it differs from our /d̶/ in that the Spanish articulation is distinctly alveolar (rather than interdental). The acoustic result is less audible friction than in English. Compare the postvocalic sound in Spanish **padre** with its counterpart in **father**.

In such endings as **-do** or **-da** and in word-final position before a pause, the sound /d̶/ is considerably unvoiced and sometimes almost inaudible. This phonetic phenomenon is represented by a subliteral diacritic: **dado** [dad̶o], **estimada** /estimad̶a/, **usted** /usted̶/, **verdad** /berdad̶/.

The sound of English /v/ as in **vine** does not occur in Spanish. The letter **v,** preserved in spelling mainly for historic reasons, is pronounced either /b/ or /b̶/.

Many speakers of Spanish do not have in their consonant system the /h/ of **he** or **him**. The letter **h** as in **ha** or **hablar** has retained its spelling for historic reasons and for visual contrast between, for example, the preposition **a** and the verb form **ha** (haber).

The palatalized /ļ/, as in the Castillian pronunciation of **calle** /kaļe/, is articulated by the lamina (not the apex) making contact with the postalveolar part of the palate. It differs from the semi-consonant /j/ in that the latter is articulated without contact between the lamina and the palate.

Semantic identity slows down the learning of certain phonological differences. Words like **nation** /nejšn/ and Spanish **nación** /nasion/ or **division** /dəvıžn/ and **división** /division/ can be profitably contrasted in sets of bilingual pairs.

Note also differences in primary stress and in the pronunciation of **s**:

ENGLISH		SPANISH	
present	/prézənt/	presente	/presénte/
president	/prézıdənt/	presidente	/presidénte/
visit	/vízıt/	visita	/visíta/
roses	/róuzız/	/rosas	/rósas/
proposition	/prapɔzıšn/	propósito	/propósito/

Vowels   Spanish vocalic sounds are articulated with more tenseness than their English counterparts. Students should be frequently reminded that Spanish has only tense, "snappy" vowels. Bilingual contrastive pairs are helpful:

ENGLISH		SPANISH	
bark	/bɑək/	barca	/bar̃ka/
cart	/kʰɑət/	carta	/kar̃ta/
Paul	/pʰɔl/	polo	/polo/
bought	/bɔt/	bota	/bota/
pest	/pʰest/	peso	/peso/
best	/best/	beso	/beso/
pick	/pʰık/	pico	/piko/
Rick	/rık/	rico	/rriko/

The tendency of students to diphthongize /o/, /e/, and /i/ in open syllables is a problem common to other foreign languages as well. A similar problem is the tendency toward vowel reduction. Students find it difficult not to reduce (slur) unstressed vowels in Spanish. The following bilingual pairs bring out this contrast:

ENGLISH		SPANISH	
parade	/pərejd/	parada	/pařada/
mural	/mjurəl/	mural	/muřal/
society	/səsajətɪ/	siciedad	/sosiedad/
correspond	/kərɛspand/	corresponder	/kořesponder/
elevate	/ɛləvejt/	elevar	/elebar/
gallery	/gælərɪ/	galería	/galeria/

It should be pointed out, however, that an occasional elimination of unaccented vowels is common in colloquial Spanish. **Qué es eso,** for example, is heard as /keseso/ and **qué va a hacer** as /kebaser/.

The glottal stop between English vowels is not used in Spanish. Instead, the speakers slightly modify one of the vowels in order to avoid ambiguity. For example, **si está** /siestá/ can be contrasted with **siesta** by pronouncing the latter /sjésta/; **no puedo ir** /nopuedoir/ can be distinguished from **no puedo oír** by lengthening, as in /nopuedo:ir/.

For a more extensive discussion of Spanish consonants and vowels, as well as their cluster, see Stockwell's *The Sounds of English and Spanish*.

In conclusion, let us return to the problem of diphthongization, the tendency to turn certain tense vowels (in open syllables) into diphthongs. This peculiarity of the English sound system leads students to hear the sounds /i/, /e/, and /o/ as diphthongs whenever they occur in open syllables. (Note, however, that the foreign lax vowels /ɪ/, /ɛ/, /ɔ/ are heard as familiar nondiphthongized vowels of English.)

The natural propensity of English speakers to glide from an open vowel to the sound /j/ or /u/ can be counteracted by contrasting bilingual pairs such as the following:

ENGLISH	FRENCH		ENGLISH	FRENCH	
fee	fit	/fi/	foe	faux	/fo/
see	si	/si/	doe	dos	/do/
me	mis	/mi/	so	sot	/so/
day	des	/de/	bow	beau	/bo/
Fay	fée	/fe/	mow	mot	/mo/

Correction of the diphthongized /o/ in open syllables of French can also be obtained in utterances with rising intonation:

Quel château?   C'est beau?   Trop tôt?
C'est haut?   C'est faux?   Quel bateau?

ENGLISH	GERMAN	ENGLISH	GERMAN
fee	Vieh /fi:/	boat	Boot /bo:t/
Dee	die /di:/	note	Not /no:t/
gai	gehe! /ge:/	tone	Ton /to:n/
Dane	den /de:n/	mode	Mode /mo:də/

ENGLISH	SPANISH	ENGLISH	SPANISH
me	mi /mi/	low	lo /lo/
see	si /si/	no	no /no/
Kay	que /ke/	cone	con /kon/
day	de /de/	dose	dos /dos/

Students who diphthongize interconsonantal vowels in Spanish should be advised to listen for the sounds of their /ɛ/ and /ɔ/, which are generally more acceptable than the diphthongs. They may benefit from bilingual pairs such as these:

ENGLISH	SPANISH	ENGLISH	SPANISH
mess	mesa /mesa/	law	loco /loko/
pest	pesca /peska/	ball	bobo /bobo/

Similarly, to counteract the tendency to substitute /ou/ for /o/ in Spanish, and to prevent the slurring of the final vowel, practicing words with rising intonation is suggested:

Es poco?   Es loco?   Este boche?
Es bobo?   Más pronto?   Esta noche?

The audio-lingual exercises suggested in this and preceding chapters are by no means exhaustive. More extensive series of contrastive pairs and triplets can be found in various drill books specifically concerned with the improvement of pronunciation.

All languages are spoken in pluralistic societies and no single "correct" speech can be claimed by any group or region. Native speakers everywhere have the tendency to change certain of their pronunciation habits from time to time. It is, therefore, important that phonetic information and materials be constantly reviewed.

7 PRACTICAL HINTS: MORPHOPHONEMICS AND SYNTAX

PATTERN DRILLS

Language, according to Chomsky, is rule-governed creative behavior. We communicate in our native language through an intricate system of patterns without awareness of the nature of these patterns. We manipulate these patterns mechanically, almost unconsciously. The native speaker has internalized the patterns of his language in the process of growing up, sometime between the ages of two and eight.

Most students in beginning a second or third language have already passed that ideal age at which linguistic memory reaches its peak. Nevertheless, one aim of basic language instruction should be to attain the same kind of automatic control, the same internalization of morphophonemic and syntactic patterns inherent in the speech of a native speaker.

Control of a foreign language can be achieved by oral exercises called pattern drills. In a pattern drill, the student receives appropriate cues which elicit responses patterned after a previously heard model. Each pattern drill is designed to help him acquire the mastery of a particular morphophonemic or grammatical item by providing sufficient opportunity for repetition of the item in a variety of utterances.

MORPHOPHONEMIC DRILLS

Drills with minimal pairs, like those in the preceding chapter, were based on the linguistic concept of *allophones*. Drills on morphophonemic items are based largely on the concept of *allomorphs*.

In Chapter 6, we observed that native speakers use one allophone of a given phoneme in a certain phonemic context and shift to another allophone when the context changes. In Spanish, for example, the velar stop /g/ is used at the beginning of an utterance (after a pause in speaking), as in **goma** or **gardía.** If, however, a word starting with /g/ occurs within a chain of sounds, the sound /g/ alternates with its fricative counterpart /g̶/, depending on what precedes. Thus, **un gato** contains /g/, but **mi gato** or **la goma** contains /g̶/.

This is the sort of simple morphophonemic change that can frequently be observed in English: **the** (/də/) **book** as against **the** (/di/) **old book.**

We will limit our discussion of drills dealing with such changes to a few samples representative of the principle. In the samples below, the student is drilled in the use of the two phonemic shapes of the definite plural article in French. The instructions are to change singular to plural. Cues can be relatively long, since they may also serve to give the student practice in listening to rapid utterances. Responses should be equally rapid:

MODEL: *Cue*	la maison noire	*Student*	les maisons noires /lemezõnwaːʀ/
	l'usine noire		les usines noires /lezyzinwaːʀ/
DRILL	la gare fermée		les gares fermées
	l'école fermée		les écoles fermées
	la route illuminée		les routes illuminées
	l'avenue illuminée		les avenues illuminées
	la maison blanche		les maison blanches
	l'église blanche		les églises blanches

The following is a sample of a drill on the two phonemic shapes of a French pronoun: /ilz/ in a prevocalic position and /il/ in a preconsonantal position. The instructions are the same as above:

MODEL RESPONSES: ils regardent /ilʀəgaʀd/
ils écoutent /ilzekut/

Cue	il parle	*Student*	ils parlent
	il examine		ils examinent
	il regarde		ils regardent

il apporte	ils apportent
il affiche	ils affichent

A somewhat more demanding drill would involve, for example, French verbs of the -**ir** class or irregular verbs requiring two changes in the response:

Cue Il élargit le jardin.   *Student* Ils élargissent le jardin.
    /**i**lelaʀžiləžaʀdẽ/   /**ilz**elaʀ**ž**isləžaʀdẽ/

The same principle applies to the drilling of verb inflections in other languages:

Cue Ich gehe weg.   *Student* Wir gehen weg.
    /ixgeəvɛk/   /virgeə**n**vɛk/
    Ich gebe es weg.   Wir geben es weg.
    Ich brauche Geld.   Wir brauchen Geld.
    Ich rauche Zigarretten.   Wir rauchen Zigarretten.

Cue Estoy en casa.   Estamos en casa.
    /estojenkasa/   /est**amos**enkasa/
    Voy a Madrid.   Vamos a Madrid.
    Hablo a Juan.   Hablamos a Juan.
    Trabajo en Madrid.   Trabajamos en Madrid.

Cue Он читает по-русски.   Они читают по-русски.
    /an**č**itájətparuski/   /a**ņ**ičitáj**ut**paruski/
    Он работает в лаборатории.   Они работают в лаборатории.
    Он понимает по-французски.   Они понимают по-французски.
    Он играет в щскоце.   Они играют в щкоце.

Similar drills may be constructed for other inflectional forms of verbs as well as for the particular phonemic shapes of the future, conditional, and simple past tenses. The difficulty of the drills can be increased by introducing less frequent verbs. The student need not know the meaning of all the verbs as long as he knows the meaning of the morphophonemic changes he is performing.

Note that in this category of drills the student practices morphophonemic alterations, while word order remains unchanged.

SYNTACTIC DRILLS

Syntactic pattern drills are based on sentence patterns and sentence transformations. Such drills are also designed to reveal a basic pattern of constant syntactic relationships while lexical elements are interchangeable. The student must perceive the similarity of structure underlying a given number of semantically different messages. Through analogy, he is then expected to apply the recognized structure to other sentences that differ in content but have the same structural characteristics.

Substitution   Each sentence pattern or frame has a certain number of slots which can be filled with interchangeable items. The interchange or substitution may take place either in one particular slot throughout a given drill, or it may progress from one slot to another. Thus, we distinguish a simple substitution and a progressive substitution.

Foreign-language sentences whose structures parallel English are no problem. In syntax, as much as in phonology, we concentrate on so-called points of conflict, structures which are unfamiliar or non-existent in the student's native language. For example, in English, "we ask someone for something," in French, "on demande quelque-chose à quelqu'un," and in German, "man verlangt etwas von jemandem." We say "He will like the general arrangement better," but in French, Russian, German, or Spanish, the sequence of corresponding lexical units is quite different.

In a foreign language, a frequent point of syntactic conflict is the order of pronouns within a sentence. English pronouns simply take the place of nouns without any change in structure. (A notable exception occurs in such sentences as: "I looked up **the word** — I looked **it** up.") A familiar pronoun substitution in a basic sentence, exemplifying the pattern N — v — V — N, is this:

> I have seen **the film.**
> I have seen **it.**

Lower case "v" in the above pattern stands for "auxiliary verb." The pattern can generate many sentences by admitting into either of the two "N" slots a large number of nouns or pronouns and by allowing the "V" slot to be filled with a large number of transitive verbs.

The pattern N — N — v — V, unfamiliar in English, is very common in French: **Je l'ai vu.** To master this pattern, students require a drill in which the appropriate forms of the past participles fill the verb slots. In this way, students learn the new pattern subconsciously while concentrating on the necessary changes in the verb form:

Teacher	je — acheter	*Student*	je l'ai acheté
	entendre		je l'ai entendu
	nous — apporter		nous l'avons apporté
	finir		nous l'avons fini

The same process occurs with the German pattern N — v — N — V:

Teacher	ich — sehen	*Student*	ich habe es gesehen
	schreiben		ich habe es geschrieben
	wir — suchen		wir haben es gesucht
	finden		wir haben es gefunden

Similarly, the unfamiliar pattern typical of French and Spanish sentences with direct and indirect object pronouns:

Teacher	je — lui — donner	*Student*	je le lui ai donné
	vendre		je le lui ai vendu
	nous — leur — montrer		nous le leur avons montré
	rendre		nous le leur avons rendu

Teacher	yo — dar	*Student*	se lo he dado
	vender		se lo he vendido
	nosotros — mandar		se lo habemos mandado
	devolver		se lo habemos devuelto

In German, such structures as **Ich habe es ihm kaufen müssen** (I had to buy it for him) can also be internalized by a substitution drill:

| *Teacher* | ich — kaufen | *Student* | ich habe es ihm kaufen müssen |
| | bringen | | ich habe es ihm bringen müssen |

wir — schreiben	wir haben es ihm
	schreiben müssen
sagen	wir haben es ihm sagen
	müssen

Observe that the cues in the above drill samples are short, so as not to give away the syntax of the responses. The samples with verb cues require the student to concentrate on the morphophonemic change in the responses (the past participle) and help him to internalize the new structure. The German sample, however, presents a structural conflict that requires concentration on syntax alone.

Progressive Substitution   Familiarity with the lexical elements of a progressive substitution drill is important. The student must not only know the meaning of the words but also recognize their grammatical category. Another factor is that some of the cues are apt to elicit more than one correct response. This makes the drill less suitable for chorus practice. The following are sketches of a substitution drill in French and Spanish:

Base sentence   Je viens toujours en retard. (I always come late.)

	Cue		*Student*	
	à midi		Je viens toujours à midi.
	souvent		Je viens souvent à midi.
	mange		Je mange souvent à midi.
	nous		Nous mangeons souvent à midi.
	trop tard		Nous mangeons souvent trop tard.
	toujours		Nous mangeons toujours trop tard.

Base sentence   El no conoce a ese señor. (He does not know this gentleman.)

	Cue		*Student*	
	hombre		El no conoce a ese hombre.
	se parece		El no se parece a ese hombre.
	nosotros		Nosotros no nos parecemos a ese hombre. (Also: El no se parece a nosotros.)

To avoid the ambiguity of the last cue, **nosotros no** might replace **nosotros.**

Expansion   If the exercise involves progressive adding of words to the base sentence, it is an expansion drill. The following is a sample in French:

Base sentence   J'ai vu mon camarade. (I have seen my friend.)

Cue	souvent	*Student*	J'ai souvent vu mon camarade.
	au cinéma		J'ai souvent vu mon camarade au cinéma.
	bon		J'ai souvent vu mon bon camarade au cinéma.

The aim of the drill is to teach students to place the cue in the appropriate slot within a given sentence.

Transformation   Sentences are transformed by making them negative, interrogative, or imperative, or by changing their mood, voice, aspect, or tense. An exercise based on such sentence changes is called a transformation drill. It may be designed in several ways. For example, the student is instructed to make negative the affirmative utterances given as cues:

| *Cue* | Il fait du bruit. | *Student* | Il ne fait pas de bruit. |
| | (He makes noise.) | | (He does not make noise.) |

Interrogative forms may be elicited by cue statements for which the student is to provide questions. Examples in French and German are:

Cue	Elle pense à Roger.	*Student*	A qui pense-t-elle?
	Roger pense à ses vacances.		A quoi pense Roger?
	Er denkt daran.		Woran denkt er?
	Sie fragt mich.		Wen fragt sie?

The imperative (or negative imperative) may be cued by instructions such as "Tell me to (or not to)." Example:

Cue	to open the door for you	*Student*	Open the door for me.
	to bring you the book		Bring me the book.
	not to look at you		Don't look at me.

Many transformations are effected through combining two utterances into one:

| The man left. | |
| The man was kind. | The kind man left. |

This kind of transformation is often called integration. Following are a few samples of integration drills to practice the structures of relative clauses and adverbial clauses:

Cue	The man called. The man was his friend.	*Student*	The man who called was his friend.
	Conozco al profesor. Vive en Barcelona.		Conozco al profesor que vive en Barcelona.
	Vi al hombre. Vd. le dio la carta.		Vi al hombre a quien Vd. dio la carta.
	The sun was shining. The farmers worked.		The farmers worked while the sun was shining.
	Marie préparait le repas. J'écrivais des lettres.		J'écrivais des lettres pendant que Marie préparait le repas.

The subjunctive mood can be cued by similar pairs of basic sentences to be integrated into one:

Cue	Il faut partir. Vous partez.	*Student*	Il faut que vous partiez.
	Il est malade. Je ne le crois pas.		Je ne crois pas qu'il soit malade.
	Es culpable. Lo dudo.		Dudo que sea culpable.
	Tiene hambre. Eso es triste.		Es triste que tenga hambre.

It is quicker, however, to practice the subjunctive by following this type of drill:

Cue	il faut	*Student*	
	—vous partez		Il faut que vous partiez.
	—nous le faisons		Il faut que nous le fassions.
	je ne crois pas		Je ne crois pas qu'il soit malade.
	—il est malade		
	—vous avez raison		Je ne crois pas que vous ayez raison.

dudo

—es culpable	Dudo que sea culpable.
—trata de creer	Dudo que trate de creer.

es lástima	Es lástima que tenga
—tiene hambre	hambre.
—no se alegra	Es lástima que no se alegre.

The devices used to construct syntactic pattern drills are many. Some of them are time-consuming for the teacher and somewhat puzzling to the student, but there are times when a drill will yield better results than other methods.

Not every drill represents an exercise in morphophonemic or syntactic change. Some are simply designed to practice vocabulary or to simulate conversation. For example, in the so-called *rejoinder drill* the student is told how to respond to a given statement:

Agree	It's a nice day.	*Student*	Yes it is.
	He is a good man.		Yes he is.
Disagree	I like the film.		I don't.
	I am satisfied.		I am not.

In a *completion drill,* the student is asked to supply an appropriate word to complete a statement:

Cue He likes his parents and you like...
Student He likes his parents and you like yours.

Cue El ama a sus padres y tú amas a...
Student El ama a sus padres y tú amas a los tuyos.

Obviously, a great deal of oral training can be achieved by means other than pattern drills. They are, however, uniquely suitable for the practice of unfamiliar sentence structures. In substitution drills we have to be careful, for each language has structure slots that cannot be indiscriminately filled with any noun, verb, or other lexical item. For example, in the pattern N — V (transitive) — N we can use "The horse kicked the man," but we cannot substitute **dog** for **horse,** even though both are four-legged animals. As was pointed out in Chapter 4, sentence structure and word meaning are frequently interdependent.

The Mechanics of Pattern Drills   The following are some general rules for conducting a pattern drill:

Explain briefly the aim of each drill and the procedures to be followed.

Keep utterances short; avoid extraneous vocabulary.

Devise a system of hand signals (*start, stop, repeat, louder,* etc.) to avoid words that might interfere with the items of the drill.

Follow the students' responses with correct responses for reinforcement.

Have students repeat correct responses, and occasionally call for individual responses.

Generally, drills should be presented in two phases. The first phase prepares the student for each new stimulus or cue by analogy with the preceding example. This phase involves a number of utterances of the same category. The second phase follows without any signal that it is a different part of the drill. It represents a sampling in random order of the various items introduced systematically during the first phase. If, for example, the drill is on the use of the Spanish indirect object pronoun, the following is a representative sketch of its details:

Replace the last word of each sentence by the appropriate indirect object pronoun:

Example	*Cue*	Roberto habla a su padre
	Response	Roberto le habla
Continue	*C.*	Roberto escribe a su hermano
	R.	. . . . . .
	Confirm.	Roberto le escribe (Pause for voluntary repeat)
	C.	Roberto habla a su madre
	R.	. . . . . .
	Confirm.	Roberto le habla (Pause)

> Six more utterances eliciting the use of **le** in the response. Each response is followed by a confirmation and a pause for a repeat.

Example   *C.*   Roberto habla a sus padres
                R.   Roberto les habla

Continue   *C.*   Roberto escribe a sus hermanas
                R.   . . . . . .
                Confirm.   Roberto les escribe (Pause)

Seven more utterances eliciting the use of **les**, following the above procedure.

(Testing)   María habla a su hermano
                 . . . . . .   (María le habla)
                 Roberto habla a sus hermanos
                 . . . . . .   (Roberto les habla)
                 El padre escribe a Roberto
                 . . . . . .   (El padre le escribe)

The same drill can be employed for the practice of pronouns in the other foreign languages. Here are shortened examples:

French   *C.*   Robert parle à son père
             R.   . . . .
             Conf.   Robert lui parle (Pause)

                   Robert parle à ses parents
                   . . . .
                   Robert leur parle (Pause)

German   *C.*   Ich zeige es dem Vater
             R.   . . . .
             Conf.   Ich zeige es ihm (Pause)

                   Ich zeige es der Mutter
                   . . . .
                   Ich zeige es ihr (Pause)

Russian   *C.*   Иван говорит с отцом
             R.   . . . .
             Conf.   Иван с ним говорит   (Pause)

                   Иван говрит с матерью
                   . . . .
                   Иван с ней говорит   (Pause)

To sum up, a pattern drill consists of a number of meaningful utterances of the same morphophonemic or syntactic pattern. The purpose of a drill is to reveal the consistency of the pattern and to help the student internalize it. To internalize is to reach the point of associating a thought directly with the sounds, morphology, and syntax of the foreign language, thereby overcoming the habits already developed in one's native language.

Drills conducted by a well-prepared teacher enable students also to observe the facial expressions and gestures appropriate for certain utterances. Classroom time, however, should be devoted primarily to other learning experiences designed to counterbalance the routine of audio-lingual drills.

Drills done as part of regular classroom instruction are chiefly an introduction to more extensive drill work in a language laboratory.

SOME NOTES ON LANGUAGE LABORATORIES

The significant advantage of a laboratory is that students, isolated by earphones, are not influenced by the nonnative utterances of their classmates and are not limited to hearing only the voice of their teacher. The laboratory and adapted teaching materials are also an effective aid for audio-lingual self-instruction.

The most elementary language-laboratory equipment consists of a tape player, which is the distributor of audio material, and of a network of wiring which carries the material to a pair of earphones provided for each student. The wiring between the tape player and the earphones can be eliminated if the amplifiers of the earphones are powered by batteries attached to each earphone headset. The tape player in this case is connected to a kind of closed-circuit radio, which broadcasts the material into the students' earphones. Both these situations represent the use of electronic devices constituting the so-called *audio-passive laboratory*.

The addition of a microphone, which enables the student to hear his voice conducted electronically to his earphones, constitutes an *audio-active laboratory*. The microphone can be a separately wired piece of equipment, or it can be attached to the earphone headset. If attached, it is called a boom-type microphone.

A laboratory in which the students have not only earphones and microphones but also individual tape recorders is known as a *listen-record laboratory*.

Tape recorders installed in the students' positions (booths) constitute a *manual control system*. This system is seldom without a monitoring console, which can have several tape players and one or more record players, making it possible to provide a number of programs simultaneously. The typical console has a switchboard that enables the instructor or an attendant to channel the audio material of the several programs to any combination of student positions. Furthermore, the instructor at the console can monitor any student and have a two-way conversation with him without disrupting others. At the console, the student can also be recorded for later evaluation, provided one of the tape players is also a tape recorder electronically connected with the switchboard.

If the students' tape recorders are installed in a special room, which may be any distance from the language laboratory proper, we speak about a *remote control system*. The tape recorders are usually stacked on movable metal racks and are not accessible to the students. The desirable aspect of this system is the simple manner of operation. The students don headsets, push a button and listen to the material from one of the tracks of the remote tape. They respond following the stimuli and can record their voices on the other track of that tape. When the lesson is completed, the tape is automatically rewound and replayed. Each student can advance or stop his remote tape electronically.

To insure privacy for the learner, various types of semi-isolated booths are commonly used as student positions. Recently, some schools started using a sound-proof cabin, which looks like a telephone booth, equipped with a loudspeaker and a microphone. There is no headset for the student and there are no moving parts to distract him while he works. There is only a dial or a push button to contact an automated tape center and to select the desired lesson, which is then channeled into the loudspeaker of the cabin.

Language laboratories may be divided into three general types:

The classroom setup typically involves a situation in which the equipment is used by one class at a time. Occasionally, "a class" represents several sections of the same course. With manual-control, listen-record equipment, which is most common in this setup, students either find a tape already on the tape recorder or put on their own tape. Then they don headsets and turn on the machines, following the signal by the instructor. They record the audio material channeled from the master tape (or a record) being played on the console. They listen, repeat, and respond, and may or may not record their own voices. If they brought their own tape, they will have a copy of the master tape for individual practice outside the laboratory.

The library setup is an installation in which students come in as they would to a library and use the laboratory equipment independently of their classmates. Since the instructors of the various courses are not present, the students are guided by a program schedule set up for each week in connection with their work in class. Depending on the equipment available, there are two basic uses of the library setup:

(a) If the booths are not equippped with tape recorders, the audio material is channeled to each booth from a console or from a remote tape center, where an attendant plays master tapes on as many tape players as are necessary for the lessons on any given day. For example, if on Monday morning an elementary and an intermediate lesson in four different languages are to be offered, eight master-tape players will be needed. Either the students of the different courses are directed to particular booths preset for their program or, in some laboratories, they sit where they choose and select their program by dialing a code number on a device installed in the booth.

(b) If the booths are equipped with tape recorders, the laboratory usually contains shelves with appropriately labeled lesson tapes. (In some cases the students have their private copies of the lesson tapes.) A student may come when he is free, check out a tape (or use his own) according to his program schedule, place it on the tape recorder, and do the assigned work. When the assignment is finished, the borrowed tape is returned to the shelf as one would return a book "on reserve."

The multiple residence setup includes several residence halls electronically linked with an audio-material distribution center, typically housed in the campus radio station. This center maintains a battery of automated, self-rewinding tape players, capable of continuous remote-control service. Students stay in their residence halls and use their own room or a designated area, equipped with audio-passive, audio-active, or listen-record facilities. The audio material in the distribution center is organized by instructors in charge of the different courses and is made available according to a weekly program schedule.

So much for a general description of the classroom, the library, and the residence laboratory setups. What are their main advantages and disadvantages?

On the secondary level, there are distinct advantages in the classroom-type setup. The teachers know that all students in a given course will have done the laboratory exercises as scheduled and under competent supervision. Teachers can easily check attendance and the quality of the work done in the laboratory. They see to it that equipment is not abused and that irrelevant behavior is ruled out. They monitor individual students and interject corrections and suggestions. The majority of students prefer working in the laboratory with a monitor and with their own classmates.

The disadvantage of this setup is that, even if a class were to use the laboratory only once a week, no more than forty class groups can be accommodated during the usual day-class hours in a five-day week. Today, many schools have more than forty foreign-language classes claiming the use of the laboratory.

The advantage of the library setup is that it normally permits a large number of students, at different proficiency levels, to do laboratory work at their own pace. They may come to the laboratory whenever it is open. Slower students may stay longer and come more often. Supervision may be by persons below the rank of teacher.

A disadvantage is the problem of attendance and of "rush hours." Students come for their assignments and find the laboratory full. They may use this as an excuse for not coming again, even though at other times the room might be half-empty. Time cards and similar devices are necessary to assure required attendance.

In the multiple residence setup the obvious advantage is the relative privacy and convenience for resident students. The disadvantage is the unavailability of the equipment to nonresident students and the recurring problem of coordinating classroom instruction with the preset program schedule of the audio-material distribution center.

By and large, despite occasional articles cautioning against an over-mechanization of the language-teaching process, the profession has now recognized the language laboratory as an effective tool.[1]

[1] Regarding audio-visual equipment, the most important technical develop-ments are in the field of the cartridged sound-film projectors. The cartridged sound film permits repetitive showings of up to fifteen or twenty-minute sequences. The special projector is small enough to be used by the student in his booth. There are as yet, however, few such films for the different levels of language competency. A similar lack of suitable materials has been hamper-ing the use of closed-circuit television in students' booths.

GLOSSARY

The following items supplement the terms employed and explained in the text:

Absorption: The suppression of a sound or its incorporation into an immediately following or preceding sound.

Accentuation: The word stress on a certain syllable of a given word.

Accusative: The case form of a noun, adjective, or pronoun, signaling the grammatical object of the sentence.

Acoustic Phonetics: A branch of physics which describes the physical qualities of speech sounds.

Agglutinative Language: A language combining various linguistic elements in a single word.

Alliteration: The repeated occurrence of a sound or cluster of sounds in succeeding words.

Allokine: A member of a kineme. Analogous to allophone.

Alternants: Allomorphs or phonemic shapes of the same morpheme.

Applied Linguistics: A discipline which seeks the solution of language-learning problems by a practical application of certain ideas developed by linguistics proper.

Aspect: A grammatical category indicating whether the action or state denoted by a verb is regarded as momentary, enduring, to continue or to be terminated in the future.

Assonance: The repetition of vocalic sounds.

Asyllabic: A phoneme which cannot be a syllable by itself.

Atonic: Without stress or pitch.

Binary: Consisting of two elements or two characteristics.

Case: A morphological variant of a noun, adjective, pronoun, or numeral. The syntactical relationship of a word indicated by a preposition, suffix, or word order.

Church-Slavonic: A South Slavic language used by Kyrillos and Methodos in translating the Gospels (9th century A.D.).

Closed Syllable: A syllable ending in a consonant.

Colloquialism: An informal expression or linguistic form, generally reserved for informal speech.

Compound: A compound word, composed of two or more words. The meaning of a compound may be different from that of the individual components.

Congruence: Morphological or other agreement.

Conjugate: To use inflections in order to express various persons, numbers, tenses, etc. of a verb.

Culture: The artistic achievements and social behavior patterns of a language community.

Direct Method: A method of teaching a foreign language through conversation without the use of the student's native language or grammatical explanations. The first words are taught by pointing to objects, pictures, or by performance.

Dialect: A variety of a given language, spoken by only a segment of the total language community.

FLES: Initials of Foreign Language in Elementary Schools.

Grapheme: A written symbol representing a speech sound.

Guttural: A synonym of velar (a consonant articulated by the back of the tongue against the velum).

Homograph: Two or more words alike in spelling but different in pronunciation, as the verb *separate* and the adjective *separate*.

Homonym: A word having the same pronunciation and spelling as another, but differing from it in meaning, as *pool* (water) and *pool* (game).

Homophone: A word having the same pronunciation as another but different from it in spelling, as *dog's* and *dogs*. Also two or more sounds which differ only in the way they are represented in spelling, as *f* and *ph*.

Idiolect: The speech pattern or habits of one individual.

Intransitive Verb: A verb not having a direct object, as *belong, go, seem*.

Kine: The smallest unit of perceivable action (gesticulation). Analogous to *phone.*

Kineme: A class of kines which may be substituted for each other without changing the significance of a perceivable unit in a gestural motion of one body area. Analogous to *phoneme.*

Kinemorph: A sequence of gestural motion particles from more than one body area.

Langue: A term proposed by Ferdinand de Saussure, a Swiss linguist (1857–1913), to describe the institutional aspects of speech which can be shared by all members of a speech community. Learning a language in a classroom situation is normally the study of the *langue.* (See also *Parole.*)

Lexicography: Listing and describing the words or morphemes of a language.

Lexicology: The study of the words of a language.

Normative: Refers to procedures that tend to prescribe what *should* be said, rather than what *is* said by native speakers.

Obstruant: A consonant articulated by partial obstruction of the flow of air (a fricative), or a complete obstruction (a stop).

Occlusive: A consonant articulated by a stop (an occlusion) of the flowing air. The manner in which a consonant is produced.

Off-glide: The reduced vocalic sound that native speakers of English regularly add to many vowels, converting them into diphthongs.

Paralinguistics: The study of paralanguage, that is, vocal qualifiers which are not classified as suprasegmental phonemes: tone of voice, drawling. etc. Also the study of nonvocal communication: hand gestures, facial expressions, etc.

Parole: A term designating the innovational aspect of speech which lends itself to modification by individual speakers. Picking up a language outside of school just by being with its native speakers may be called learning the *parole.* (See also *Langue.*)

Phsycholinguistics: The study of language as learned behavior and as a structured system of signs. Combines the endeavors of linguists and psychologists.

Resonant: A vowel or a consonant produced by shaping but not obstructing the sound carrying air (m, n, ŋ, l, r). Synonym of *sonant* or *sonorant.*

Schwa: A Hebrew term used to describe the reduced vowel sound represented by /ə/.

Synchronic Linguistics: The study of a language at the present moment in its development.

Transliteration: Representation or spelling in the characters of another alphabet. For instance, Russian words are transliterated with the letters of the Latin alphabet. There is no official system of transliterating Russian characters. Most libraries and newspapers follow the system initiated by the Library of Congress, which is that used in this book. There is also a system called morpho-phonemic transliteration. It uses the symbols of a phonemic alphabet while keeping conventional spacing between words.

Word Frequency: A count of the frequency with which words appear in samples of speech or writing. Such counts are useful to guide us in selecting vocabulary to be included in conversation exercises.

BIBLIOGRAPHY

This bibliography is designed as a survey of some of the basic works recently published in the field of linguistics.

The listing excludes writings which belong to a more advanced or more specialized level of study.

Materials available from the MLA-ACTFL Materials Center (62 Fifth Avenue, New York, N.Y. 10011) are not listed here, since updated listings of materials may be periodically obtained directly from the Center.

ANTHOLOGIES

Abercrombie, David, *Studies in Phonetics and Linguistics*. London: Oxford University Press, 1965.

Allen, Harold B. (ed.), *Applied English Linguistics*. 2nd ed.; New York: Appleton-Century-Crofts, 1964.

Belasco, Simon (ed.), *Anthology*. Boston: D. C. Heath, 1961.

Dean, Leonard F., and Wilson, K. G., *Essays on Language and Usage*, 2nd ed.; New York: Oxford University Press, 1963.

Lenneberg, Eric H. (ed.), *New Directions in the Study of Language*. Cambridge, Mass.,: M.I.T. Press, 1966.

Levenson, Stanley, and Kendrick, W., *Readings in Foreign Languages for the Elementary School*. Waltham, Mass.: Blaisdell, 1967.

Libbish, B. (ed.), *Advances in the Teaching of Modern Languages*. New York: Macmillan, 1964. Vol. 1.

Michel, Joseph, *Foreign Language Teaching*. New York: Macmillan, 1967.

Roucek, Joseph S. (ed.) *Study of Foreign Languages*. New York: Philosophical Library, 1968.

Saporta, Sol (ed.), *Psycholinguistics: A Book of Readings*. New York: Holt, Rinehart and Winston, 1961.

173

Strevens, Peter, *Papers in Language and Language Teaching*. London: Oxford University Press, 1965.

Valdman, Albert (ed.), *Trends in Language Teaching*. New York: McGraw-Hill, 1966.

GENERAL

Bach, Emmon, *An Introduction to Transformational Grammars*. New York: Holt, Rinehart and Winston, 1964.

Barber, Charles, *The Flux of Language*. London: George Allen and Unwin Ltd., 1965

Bennett, William A., *Aspects of Language and Language Teaching*. New York: Cambridge University Press, 1968.

Bloomfield, Leonard, *Language*. New York: Holt, 1933.

Brooks, Nelson, *Language and Language Learning*, 2nd. ed. New York: Harcourt, Brace and World, 1964.

Brown, Marshall L., and White, Elmer, *Grammar for English Sentences*. Columbus, Ohio: Charles E. Merrill Books, Inc., 1966.

Carroll, John B., *The Study of Language, A Survey of Linguistics and Related Disciplines in America*. Cambridge, Mass.: Harvard U. Press, 1955.

Catford, J. C., *Linguistic Theory of Translation*. London: Oxford U. Press, 1965.

Chomsky, Noam, *Current Issues in Linguistic Theory*. The Hague: Mouton, 1964.

————, *Syntactic Structures*. The Hague: Mouton & Co., 1961.

Cornfield, Ruth R., *Foreign Language Instruction. Dimensions and Horizons*. New York: Appleton-Century-Crofts, 1966.

Dunkel, Agard, *An Investigation of Second-Language Learning*. Boston: Ginn, 1948.

Elson, Benjamin and Pickett, Velma, *An Introduction to Morphology and Syntax*. California: Summer Institute of Linguistics, 1967.

Etmekjian, James, *Pattern Drills in Language Teaching*. New York: New York U. Press, 1966.

Firth, J. R., *The Tongues of Men and Speech*. New York: Oxford U. Press, 1964.

Fries, Charles C., *Linguistics, The Study of Language*. New York: Holt, Rinehart and Winston, Inc., 1965.

————, *The Structure of English*. New York: Harcourt Brace, 1952.

————, *Teaching and Learning English as a Foreign Language*. Ann Arbor: U. of Michigan, 1945.

Gage, William W., *Contrastive Studies in Linguistics*. New York: Center for Applied Linguistics, 1961.

Gleason, Henry A. Jr., *An Introduction to Descriptive Linguistics*. (Rev. ed.). New York: Holt, Rinehart and Winston, 1961.

———, *Linguistics and English Grammar*. New York: Holt, Rinehart and Winston, 1965.

Gouin, François, *The Art of Teaching and Studying Languages*, 5th ed. Trans. by H. Swan and V. Betis. London: Philip & Son, 1896.

Hall, Edward T., *The Silent Language*. New York: Doubleday & Co., 1959.

Hall, Robert A., *Introductory Linguistics*. Philadelphia: Chilton Books, 1964.

———, *Linguistics & Your Language*. New York: Doubleday & Co., 1960.

Heffner, Roe-Merrill S., *General Phonetics*. Madison: U. of Wisconsin Press, 1949.

Hill, Archibald A., *Introduction to Linguistic Structures; from Sound to Sentence in English*. New York: Harcourt Brace, 1958.

Hjelmslev, Louis and Uldall, H. J., *Outline of Glossematics: a study in the methodology of the humanities, with special reference to linguistics*. Copenhagen: Nordisk Kulturforlag, 1957.

Hocket, Charles F., *A Course in Modern Linguistics*. New York: Macmillan, 1958.

Hocking, Elton, *Language Lab & Language Learning*. Washington, D.C.: National Educ. Assoc., 1964.

Huebener, Theodore, *How to Teach Foreign Languages Effectively*. New York: New York U. Press, 1965.

Hughes, John P., *The Science of Language; An Introduction to Linguistics*. New York: Random House, 1962.

Jakobson, Roman, and Halle, Morris, *Fundamentals of Language*. The Hague: Mouton, 1956.

Jakobson, Roman, Fant, G., and Halle, M., *Preliminaries to Speech Analysis. The distinctive features and their correlates*. Cambridge, Mass.: Acoustic Lab, M.I.T., 1952.

Jespersen, Otto, *Language; its nature, development and origin*. London: Macmillan, 1922.

Jones, Daniel, *Outline of English Phonetics*. 6th ed. New York: E. P. Duton, 1948.

Keating, R. F., *A Study of the Effectiveness of Language Laboratories*. New York: Institute of Administrative Research, Teachers College, Columbia U., 1963.

Lado, Robert, *Language Teaching*. New York: McGraw-Hill, Inc., 1964.

———. *Language Testing — The Construction and Use of Foreign Language Tests*, New York: McGraw-Hill, 1964.

————, *Linguistics Across Cultures*. Ann Arbor, Mich.: U. of Michigan Press, 1957.

Landar, Herbert, *Language and Culture*. London: Oxford U. Press, 1966.

Landers, Bertha (ed.), *Foreign Language Audio-Visual Guide*. New York: Landers Associates, 1961.

Lehman, Winfred P., *Historical Linguistics*. New York: Holt, Rinehart and Winston, 1962.

Lieberman, Philip, *Intonation, Perception, and Language*. Cambridge, Mass.: The M.I.T. Press, 1967.

Longacre, Robert E., *Grammar Discovery Procedures*. The Hague: Mouton and Co., 1964.

Mackey, William F., *Language Teaching Analysis*. London: Longmans, 1965.

Malberg, Bertil, *Phonetics*. New York: Dover Publ., 1966.

Martinet, André, *Elements of General Linguistics*. Chicago: U. of Chicago Press, 1964.

————, *A Functional View of Language*. Oxford: The Claredon Press, 1962.

Meras, Edmond A., *A Language Teacher's Guide*. New York: Harper, 1962.

Moulton, William G., *A Linguistic Guide to Language Learning*. New York: The Modern Language Association of America, 1966.

Nida, Eugene A., *Morphology: the descriptive analysis of words*. 2nd. ed., Ann Arbor: U. of Michigan Press, 1949.

Osgood, Charles E. (ed.), *Psycholinguistics; a survey of a theory and research problems*. Baltimore: Waverly Press, 1954.

Palmer, Harold E., *Principles of Language Study*. London: Oxford U. Press, 1964.

Pei, Mario, *Invitation to Linguistics*. New York: Doubleday, 1965.

————, *The Story of Language*. Philadelphia: Lippincott, 1949.

Penfield, Wilder and Roberts, Lamar, *Speech and Brain Mechanism*. Princeton: Princeton U. Press, 1959.

Perrot, Jean, *La Linguistique*. Paris: P.U. de France, 1961.

Pike, Kenneth L., *Phonemics: a technique for reducing languages to writing*. Ann Arbor: U. of Michigan Press, 1947.

————, *Phonetics*. Ann Arbor: U. of Michigan Press, 1943.

Politzer, Robert Louis, *Foreign Language Learning, A Linguistic Introduction*. Englewood Cliffs, N.J. Prentice-Hall, 1965.

Pulgram, Ernst, *Introduction to the Spectrography of Speech*. The Hague: Mouton, 1959.

Rivers, Wilga M., *Psychologist and the Foreign Language Teacher*. Chicago: U. of Chicago Press, 1964.

————, *Teaching Foreign Language Skills*. Chicago: U. of Chicago Press, 1969.

Roberts, Paul, *English Sentences*. New York: Harcourt, Brace and World, 1962.

————, *Patterns of English*. New York: Harcourt, Brace, 1956.

Robins, Robert Henry, *General Linguistics: An Introductory Survey*. Bloomington: Indiana U. Press, 1965.

Sapir, Edward, *Language*. New York: Harcourt, Brace, 1921.

Saussure, Ferdinand de, *Cours de linguistique générale*. 4th ed. Paris: Payot, 1949.

Schlauch, Margaret, *The Gift of Language*. New York: Dover Publications, Inc., 1942.

Smith, Henry Lee, Jr., *Linguistic Science and the Teaching of English*. Cambridge, Mass.: Harvard U. Press, 1956.

Spitzer, Leo, *Linguistics & Literary History*. New York: Russell & Russell, 1962.

Stageberg, Norman C., *An Introductory English Grammar*. New York: Holt, Rinehart and Winston, Inc., 1965.

Steevens, Peter D. (ed.), *Five Inaugural Lectures*. London: Oxford, 1966.

Sturtevant, Edgar H., *An Introduction to Linguistic Science*. New Haven: Yale U. Press, 1947.

Sweet, Henry, *Practical Study of Languages; A Guide for Teachers and Learners*. London: Oxford University Press, 1964.

Trager, George S., and Smith, H. S. Jr., *Outline of English Structure*. Norman: U. of Oklahoma, 1951.

Troubetzkoy, Nikolai S., *Principes de phonologie*. Trans. by J. Cantineau. Paris: Klincksieck, 1949.

Twaddel, W. Freeman, *The English Verb Auxiliaries*. Providence, R.I.: Brown U. Press, 1960.

FLES

Andersson, Theodore, *Teaching of Foreign Languages in Elementary Schools*. New York: D. C. Heath, 1963.

Erikson, Marguerite, *Foreign Languages in the Elementary School*. Englewood Cliffs, N.J.: Prentice-Hall, 1964.

Finocchiaro, Mary, *Teaching Children Foreign Languages*. New York: McGraw-Hill, 1964.

Johnston, Marjorie, *Modern Foreign Language and Your Child*. Washington, D.C.: U.S. Office of Education, 1964.

Levenson, Stanley, *Readings in Foreign Languages for the Elementary School*. Waltham, Mass.: Blaisdell, 1967.

FRENCH

Armstrong, Lilias, and Coustenoble, H., *Studies in French Intonation.* Cambridge, England: Heffer, 1934.

Armstrong, Lilias, *The Phonetics of French.* London: Bell, 1957.

Brunot, Ferdinand, *La pensée et la langue.* Paris: Masson, 1953.

Brunot, Ferdinand, and Brunneau, Charles, *Précis de grammaire historique de la langue française.* Paris: Masson & Cie., 1937.

Dauzat, Albert, *Phonétique et grammaire historiqué de la langue française.* Paris: Larousse, 1950.

Delattre, Pierre, *Les difficultés phonétique du français.* Middlebury, Vt.: Middlebury College, 1948.

——, *Principes de phonétique française.* Middlebury, Vt.: Middlebury College, 1951.

Ewert, Alfred, *The French Language.* London: Faber & Faber, 1933.

Grammont, Maurice, *Traité de phonétique.* 3e ed., rev. Paris: Delagrave, 1946.

——, *Traité pratique de prononciation française.* Paris: Delagrave, 1948.

Harmer, Lewis, C., *The French Language Today.* London: Hutchinson, 1954.

Léon, Monique, *Exercices systématiques de prononciation française.* 2 vols. Paris: Hachette, 1964.

Martinet, André, *La prononciation du français contemporain.* Paris: Droz, 1945.

Marty, Fernand, *Linguistics Applied to the Beginning French Course.* Roanoke, Virginia: Audio-Visual Publications, 1963.

Politzer, Robert L., *Teaching French: An Introduction to Applied Linguistic.* Waltham, Mass.: Blaisdell, 1965.

Pope, Mildred K., *From Latin to Modern French.* Manchester, England: Manchester U. Press, 1934.

Schane, Sanford A. *French Phonology and Morphology.* Cambridge, Mass.: M.I.T. Press, 1968.

Valdman, Albert, *Applied Linguistics: French,* (ed. Simon Belasco). Boston: D. C. Heath, 1961.

Valdman, Albert; Salazar, R. and Charbonneaux, *A Drillbook of French Pronunciation.* New York: Harper & Row, 1964.

GERMAN

Bach, Adolf, *Geschichte der deutschen Sprache.* 7th ed. Heidelberg: Quelle & Meyer, 1961.

Barker, M. L., *A Handbook of German Intonation*. Cambridge: W. Heffer & Sons Ltd., 1925.

Boost, Karl, *Neue Untersuchungen zum Wesen und zur Struktur des deutschen Satzes*. Berlin: Akademie-Verlag, 1959.

Essen, Otto von, *Allgemeine und angewandte Phonetik*. 2nd ed. Berlin: Akademie-Verlag, 1957.

————. *Grundzüge der hochdeutschen Satzintonation*. Ratingen: A. Henn Verlg., 1956.

Glinz, H., *Deutsche Syntax*. Stuttgart: Metzler, 1961.

————, *Die innere Form des Deutschen*. 2nd ed. Bern: Francke, 1961.

Hauch, E. F., *German Idiom List*. New York: Macmillan, 1931.

Kufner, Herbert L., *The Grammatical Structures of English and German*. Chicago: U. of Chicago Press, 1962.

Moulton, William G., *The Sounds of English and German*. Chicago: U. of Chicago Press, 1962.

Marchand, J. W., *Applied Linguistics: German*, (ed. Simon Belasco). Boston: D. C. Heath & Co., 1961.

Politzer, Robert L., *Teaching German, A Linguistic Orientation*. Waltham, Mass.: Blaisdell Publishing Co., 1965.

Purin, C. M., *A Standard German Vocabulary of 2,932 Words and 1,500 Idioms*. Boston: D. C. Heath, 1937.

Siebs, Theodore, *Deutsche Hochsprache, Bühnenausprache*. Berlin: W. de Gruyter, 1958.

RUSSIAN

Avanesov, Ruben J., *Fonetika sovremenovo russkovo yazika*. Moscow: Moscow U. Press, 1956.

Axmanova, O. S., *Ocherki po obshchey i russkoy leksikologii*. Moscow: 1957.

Boyanus, Semen K., *Russian Pronunciation*. Cambridge: Harvard U. Press, 1955.

Galkina, Feodor, *Sovremeniy Russkiy Yazik* (Phonology and morphology). Moscow: Moscow U. Press, 1958.

Jurgens, M. A., Buning, J. E., and Schooneveld, C. H. van, *The Sentence Intonation of Contemporary Standard Russian*. S'Gravenhage: Mouton, 1961.

Magner, Thomas F., *Applied Linguistics: Russian*. (ed. Simon Belasco.) Boston: D. C. Heath & Co., 1961.

Matthews, William K., *Structure and Development of Russian*. Cambridge: Cambridge U. Press, 1953.

Ward, Dennis, *Russian Pronunciation*. New York: Hafner, 1958.

Wolkonsky, C. and Poltoratzky, M. A., *Handbook of Russian Roots*. New York: Columbia U. Press, 1961.

SPANISH

Cardenas, Daniel N., *Applied Linguistics: Spanish*, ed. Simon Belasco. Boston: D. C. Heath & Co., 1961.

Diaz-Valenzuela, O., *The Spanish Subjunctive*. New York: David McKay Co., 1942.

Hadlich, Roger L., Holton, James S., and Montes, Matias, *A Drillbook of Spanish Pronunciation*. New York: Harper & Row, 1968.

Lapesa, Rafael, *Historia de la lengua española*. New York: Las Americas Pub. Co., 1959.

Navarro, Tomás, *Fonologia española*. Syracuse, N.Y.: Syracuse U. Press, 1946.

———, *Manuel de la pronunciación española*. New York: Hafner Pub. Co., 1957.

———. *Manuel de entonación española*. 2nd. ed. New York: Hispanic Institute, 1948.

Pidal, R. Menendez, *Manuel De Gramática histórica*. Madrid: Esposa-Calpe, 1944.

Politzer, Robert L. and Staubach, Charles N., *Teaching Spanish; A Linguistic Orientation*. Waltham, Mass.: Blaisdell, 1961.

Ramsey, Marathon M., *A Textbook of Modern Spanish*. New York: Holt, Rinehart and Winston, 1962.

Spaulding, Robt. K., *How Spanish Grew*. L. A.: U. of California Press, 1948.

Stockwell, Robert P. et al., *Grammatical Structures of English and Spanish*. Chicago: U. of Chicago Press, 1965.

Stockwell, Robert P., and Bowen J. D., *The Sounds of English and Spanish*. Chicago: U. of Chicago Press, 1965.

WORD-FREQUENCY INFORMATION

Bou, I. R.; Mendez et al., *Recuento de vocabulario español*. San Juan: U. of Puerto Rico Press, 1952.

Eaton, Helen S., *English-French-German-Spanish Word Frequency Dictionary*. New York: Dover Publications, 1940.

Josselson, Harry H., *The Russian Word Count and Frequency Analysis*. Detroit: Wayne U. Press, 1953.

Morgan, B. Q., *German Frequency Word Book*. New York: Macmillan, 1933.

West, M., Bond, O., and Limper, L. H., *A Grouped-Frequency French Word List Based on the French Word Book of Van der Beke*. Chicago: U. of Chicago Press, 1939.

PROGRAMMED LEARNING

Buchanan, Cynthia D., *A Programed Introduction to Linguistics*. Boston:
   D. C. Heath, 1965.
Carroll, John B., "Research on Teaching Foreign Languages, "in *Handbook
   of Research on Teaching*, ed. N. L. Gage. Chicago: Rand McNally, 1963.
Lumsdaine, A. A., and Glaser R., *Teaching Machines and Programed
   Learning: A Source Book*. Washington: Natl. Ed. Assoc., 1960.

ANNOTATED BIBLIOGRAPHY

Linguistic Reading List for Teachers of Modern Languages, ed. Charles A.
   Ferguson. Washington. D.C.: Center for Applied Linguistics of the MLA,
   1963.

INDEX

(Numbers refer to pages)